AMERICAN NOTES

AMERICAN NOTES

BY
RUDYARD KIPLING

BOOKS FOR LIBRARIES PRESS
FREEPORT, NEW YORK

First Published 1891
Reprinted 1972

Library of Congress Cataloging in Publication Data

Kipling, Rudyard, 1865-1936.
   American notes.

   Reprint of the 1891 ed.
   1. United States--Description and travel--1865-1900.
I. Title.
E168.K56 1972   917.3'03'88   72-5679
ISBN 0-8369-6917-0

PRINTED IN THE UNITED STATES OF AMERICA

NOTE.

THE following letters were written by **Mr.** Kipling in 1889, while on a trip from India to England by way of the United States.

They were published as special correspondence in the *Pioneer* of India at the time.

THE PUBLISHERS.

AMERICAN NOTES.

I.

" Then spoke der Captain Stossenheim
Who had theories of God,
' Oh, Breitmann, this is judgment on
Der ways dot you have trod.
You only lifs to enjoy yourself
While you yourself agree
Dot self-development requires
Der religious Idee.' "

This is America.

They call her the *City of Peking*, and she
belongs to the Pacific Mail Company, but for
all practical purposes she is the United States.

We are divided between missionaries and
generals—generals who were at Vicksburg
and Shiloh, and German by birth, but more
American than the Americans, who in confidence tell you that they are not generals at
all, but only brevet majors of militia corps.
The missionaries are perhaps the queerest
portion of the cargo. Did you ever hear an
English minister lecture for half an hour on
the freight-traffic receipts and general working

7

of, let us say, the Midland? The Professor
has been sitting at the feet of a keen-eyed,
close-bearded, swarthy man who expounded
unto him kindred mysteries with a fluency
and precision that a city leader-writer might
have envied. " Who's your financial friend
with the figures at his fingers' ends?" I
asked. " Missionary—Presbyterian Mission
to the Japs," said the Professor. I laid my
hand upon my mouth and was dumb.

As a counterpoise to the missionaries, we
carry men from Manila—lean Scotchmen who
gamble once a month in the Manila State
lottery and occasionally turn up trumps. One,
at least, drew a ten-thousand-dollar prize last
December and is away to make merry in the
New World. Everybody on the staff of an
American steamer this side the Continent
seems to gamble steadily in that lottery, and
the talk of the smoking-room runs almost
entirely on prizes won by accident or lost
through a moment's delay. The tickets are
sold more or less openly at Yokohama
and Hong-Kong, and the drawings—losers
and winners both agree here—are above reproach.

We have resigned ourselves to the infinite
monotony of a twenty days' voyage. The
Pacific Mail advertises falsely. Only under
the most favorable circumstances of wind and
steam can their under-engined boats cover
the distance in fifteen days. Our *City of*

Peking, for instance, had been jogging along at a gentle ten knots an hour, a pace out of all proportion to her bulk. " When we get a wind," says the Captain, " we shall do better." She is a four-master and can carry any amount of canvas. It is not safe to run steamers across this void under the poles of Atlantic liners. The monotony of the sea is paralyzing. We have passed the wreck of a little sealing-schooner lying bottom up and covered with gulls. She weltered by in the chill dawn, unlovely as the corpse of a man ; and the wild birds piped thinly at us as they steered her across the surges. The pulse of the Pacific is no little thing even in the quieter moods of the sea. It set our bows swinging and nosing and ducking ere we were a day clear of Yokohama, and yet there was never swell nor crested wave in sight. " We ride very high," said the Captain, " and she's a dry boat. She has a knack of crawling over things somehow ; but we shan't need to put her to the test this journey."

*   *   *   *

The Captain was mistaken. For four days we have endured the sullen displeasure of the North Pacific, winding up with a night of discomfort. It began with a gray sea, flying clouds, and a head-wind that smote fifty knots off the day's run. Then rose from the southeast a beam sea warranted by no wind that

was abroad upon the waters in our neighbor-
hood, and we wallowed in the trough of it for
sixteen mortal hours. In the stillness of the
harbor, when the newspaper man is lunching
in her saloon and the steam-launch is crawling
round her sides, a ship of pride is a " stately
liner." Out in the open, one rugged shoulder
of a sea between you and the horizon, she becomes " the old hooker," a " lively boat," and
other things of small import, for this is necessary to propitiate the Ocean. " There's
a storm to the southeast of us," explained
the Captain. " That's what's kicking up this
sea."

The *City of Peking* did not belie her repu-
tation. She crawled over the seas in liveliest
wise, never shipping a bucket till—she was
forced to. Then she took it green over the
bows to the vast edification of, at least, one
passenger who had never seen the scuppers
full before.

Later in the day the fun began. " Oh,
she's a daisy at rolling," murmured the chief
steward, flung starfish-wise on a table among
his glassware. " She's rolling some," said a
black apparition new risen from the stoke-
hold. " Is she going to roll any more? " demanded the ladies grouped in what ought to
have been the ladies' saloon, but, according to
American custom, was labeled " Social Hall."

Passed in the twilight the chief officer—a
dripping, bearded face. " Shall I mark out

the bull-board ? " said he, and lurched aft, followed by the tongue of a wave. " She'll roll her guards under to-night," said a man from Louisiana, where their river-steamers do not understand the meaning of bulwarks. We dined to a dashing accompaniment of crockery, the bounds of emancipated beer-bottles livelier than their own corks, and the clamor of the ship's gong broken loose and calling to meals on its own account.

After dinner the real rolling began. She did roll " guards under," as the Louisiana man had prophesied. At thirty-minute intervals to the second arrived one big sea, when the electric lamps died down to nothing, and the screw raved and the blows of the sea made the decks quiver. On those occasions we moved from our chairs, not gently, but discourteously. At other times we were merely holding on with both hands.

It was then that I studied Fear—Terror bound in black silk and fighting hard with herself. For reasons which will be thoroughly understood, there was a tendency among the passengers to herd together and to address inquiries to every officer who happened to stagger through the saloon. No one was in the least alarmed,—oh dear, no,—but all were keenly anxious for information. This anxiety redoubled after a more than usually vicious roll. Terror was a large, handsome, and cultured lady who knew the precise value of human life, the inwardness of *Robert Elsmere*, the latest poetry—everything in fact that a clever woman should know.   When the rolling was near its worst, she began to talk swiftly.   I do not for a moment believe that she knew what she was talking about.   The rolling increased. She buckled down to the task of making conversation.   By the heave of the laboring bust, the restless working of the fingers on the tablecloth, and the uncontrollable eyes that turned always to the companion stairhead, I was able to judge the extremity of her fear. Yet her words were frivolous and commonplace enough ; they poured forth unceasingly, punctuated with little laughs and giggles, as a woman's speech should be.   Presently, a member of her group suggested going to bed. No, she wanted to sit up; she wanted to go on talking, and as long as she could get a soul to sit with her she had her desire.   When for sheer lack of company she was forced to get to her cabin, she left reluctantly, looking back to the well-lighted saloon over her shoulder.   The contrast between the flowing triviality of her speech and the strained intentness of eye and hand was a quaint thing to behold.   I know now how Fear should be painted.

No one slept very heavily that night.   Both arms were needed to grip the berth, while the trunks below wound the carpet slips into knots and battered the framing of the cabins.   Once it seemed to me that the whole of the laboring fabric that cased our trumpery fortunes stood on end and in this undignified posture hopped a mighty hop. Twice I know I shot out of my berth to join the adventurous trunks on the floor. A hundred times the crash of the wave on the ship's side was followed by the roar of the water, as it swept the decks and raved round the deckhouses. In a lull I heard the flying feet of a man, a shout, and a far-away chorus of lost spirits singing somebody's requiem.

May 24 (Queen's Birthday).—If ever you meet an American, be good to him. This day the ship was dressed with flags from stem to stern, and chiefest of the bunting was the Union-Jack. They had given no word of warning to the English, who were proportionately pleased. At dinner up rose an ex-Commissioner of the Lucknow Division (on my honor, Anglo-India extends to the ends of the earth!) and gave us the health of Her Majesty and the President. It was afterwards that the trouble began. A small American penned half a dozen English into a corner and lectured them soundly on—their want of patriotism!

" What sort of Queen's Birthday do you call this?" he thundered. "What did you drink our President's health for? What's the President to you on this day of all others? Well, suppose you *are* in the minority, all the more reason for standing by your country.

Don't talk to me.   You Britishers made a
mess of it—a mighty bungle of the whole
thing.   I'm an American of the Americans ;
but if no one can propose Her Majesty's
health better than by just throwing it at your
heads, I'm going to try."

Then and there he delivered a remarkably
neat little oration—pat, well put together, and
clearly delivered. So it came to pass that the
Queen's health was best honored by an American. We English were dazed. I wondered
how many Englishmen not trained to addressing their fellows would have spoken half so
fluently as the gentleman from 'Frisco.

" Well, you see," said one of us feebly,
" she's our Queen, anyhow, and—and—she's
been ours for fifty years, and not one of us
here has seen England for seven years, and
we can't enthuse over the matter. We've lived
to be hauled over the coals for want of patriotism by an American !   We'll be more careful
next time."

And the conversation drifted naturally into
the question of the government of men—English, Japanese (we have several traveled Japanese aboard), and Americans throwing the
ball from one to another. We bore in mind
the golden rule : " Never agree with a man
who abuses his own country," and got on well
enough.

" Japan," said a little gentleman who was a
rich man there, " Japan is divided into two

administrative sides. On the one the remains of a very strict and quite Oriental despotism ; on the other a mass of—what do you call it ? —red-tapeism which is not understood even by the officials who handle it. We copy the red tape, and when it is copied we believe that we administer. That is a vice of all Oriental nations. We are Orientals."

" Oh no, say the most westerly of the westerns," purred an American, soothingly.

The little man was pleased. " Thanks. That is what we hope to believe, but up to the present it is not so. Look now. A farmer in my country holds a hillside cut into little terraces. Every year he must submit to his Government a statement of the size and revenue paid, not on the whole hillside, but on each terrace. The complete statement makes a pile three inches high, and is of no use when it is made except to keep in work thousands of officials to check the returns. Is that administration ? By God ! we call it so, but we multiply officials by the twenty, and *they* are not administration. What country is such a fool ? Look at our Government offices eaten up with clerks ! Some day, I tell you, there will be a smash."

This was new to me, but I might have guessed it. In every country where swords and uniforms accompany civil office there is a natural tendency towards an ill-considered increase of officialdom.

" You might pay India a visit some day," I said. " I fancy that you would find that our country shares your trouble."

Thereupon a Japanese gentleman in the Educational Department began to cross-question me on the matters of his craft in India, and in a quarter of an hour got from me the very little that I knew about primary schools, higher education, and the value of an M. A. degree. He knew exactly what he wanted to ask, and only dropped me when the tooth of desire had clean picked the bone of ignorance.

Then an American held forth, harping on a string that has already been too often twanged in my ear. " What will it be in America itself ? "

" The whole system is rotten from top to bottom," he said. " As rotten as rotten can be."

" That's so," said the Louisiana man, with an affirmative puff of smoke.

" They call us a Republic. We may be. I don't think it. You Britishers have got the only republic worth the name. You choose to run your ship of state with a gilt figurehead ; but I know, and so does every man who has thought about it, that your Queen doesn't cost you one-half what our system of pure democracy costs us. Politics in America ? There aren't any. The whole question of the day is spoils. That's all. We fight our souls out

over tram-contracts, gas-contracts, road-con-
tracts, and any darned thing that will turn a
dishonest dollar, and we call that politics.   No
one but a low-down man will run for Congress
and the Senate—the Senate of the freest
people on earth are bound slaves to some
blessed monopoly.   If I had money enough, I
could buy the Senate of the United States, the
Eagle, and the Star-Spangled Banner complete."

" And the Irish vote included ? " said some
one—a Britisher, I fancy.

" Certainly, if I chose to go yahooing down
the street at the tail of the British lion.   Anything dirty will buy the Irish vote.   That's
why our politics are dirty.   Some day you
Britishers will grant Home Rule to the vermin
in our blankets.   Then the real Americans
will invite the Irish to get up and git to where
they came from.   'Wish you'd hurry up that
time before we have another trouble.   We're
bound hand and foot by the Irish vote ; or at
least that's the excuse for any unusual theft
that we perpetrate.   I tell you there's no good
in an Irishman except as a fighter.   He doesn't
understand work.   He has a natural gift of
the gab, and he can drink a man blind.   These
three qualifications make him a first-class
politician."

With one accord the Americans present
commenced to abuse Ireland and its people as
they had met them, and each man prefaced

2

his commination service with: "I am an American by birth—an American from way back."

It must be an awful thing to live in a country where you have to explain that you really belong there. Louder grew the clamor and crisper the sentiments.

" If we weren't among Americans, I should say we were consorting with Russians," said a fellow-countryman in my ear.

" They can't mean what they say," I whispered. " Listen to this fellow."

" And I know, for I have been three times round the world and resided in most countries on the Continent, that there was never people yet could govern themselves."

" Allah! This from an American!"

" And who should know better than an American?" was the retort. " For the ignorant—that is to say for the majority—there is only one argument—fear; the fear of Death. In our case we give any scallawag who comes across the water all the same privileges that we have made for ourselves. There we make a mistake. They thank us by playing the fool. Then we shoot them down. You can't persuade the mob of any country to become decent citizens. If they misbehave themselves, shoot them. I saw the bombs thrown at Chicago when our police were blown to bits. I saw the banners in the procession that threw the bombs. All the mottoes on them were in

German. The men were aliens in our midst, and they were shot down like dogs. I've been in labor riots and seen the militia go through a crowd like a finger through tissue paper."

" I was in the riots at New Orleans," said the man from Louisiana. " We turned the Gatling on the other crowd, and they were sick."

" Whew! I wonder what would have happened if a Gatling had been used when the West End riots were in full swing ?" said an Englishman. " If a single rioter were killed in an English town by the police, the chances are that the policeman would have to stand his trial for murder and the Ministry of the day would go out."

" Then you've got all your troubles before you. The more power you give the people, the more trouble they will give. With us our better classes are corrupt and our lower classes are lawless. There are millions of useful, law-abiding citizens, and they are very sick of this thing. We execute our justice in the streets. The law courts are no use. Take the case of the Chicago Anarchists. It was all we could do to get 'em hanged; whereas the dead in the streets had been punished offhand. We were sure of *them*. Guess that's the reason we are so quick to fire on a mob. But it's unfair, all the same. We receive all these cattle—Anarchists, Socialists, and ruffians of every sort—and then we shoot them. The

States are as republican as they make 'em. We have no use for a man who wants to try any more experiments on the Constitution. We are the biggest people on God's earth. All the world knows that. We've been shouting that we are also the greatest people. No one cares to contradict us but ourselves ; and we are now wondering whether we are what we claim to be. Never mind ; you Britishers will have the same experiences to go through. You're beginning to rot now. Your County Councils will make you more rotten because you are putting power into the hands of un-trained people. When you reach our level,— every man with a vote and the right to sell it; the right to nominate fellows of his own kidney to swamp out better men,—you'll be what we are now—rotten, rotten, rotten ! "

The voice ceased, and no man rose up to contradict.

" We'll worry through it somehow," said the man from Louisiana. " What would do us a world of good now would be a big European war. We're getting slack and sprawly. Now a war outside our borders would make us all pull together. But that's a luxury we shan't get."

" Can't you raise one within your own borders ? " I said flippantly, to get rid of the thought of the great blind nation in her unrest putting out her hand to the Sword. Mine was a st unfortunate remark.

" I nope not," said an American, very seriously. " We have paid a good deal to keep ourselves together before this, and it is not likely that we shall split up without protest. Yet some say we are too large, and some say that Washington and the Eastern States are running the whole country. If ever we do divide,—God help us when we do,—it will be East and West this time."

" We built the old hooker too long in the run. Put the engine-room aft. Break her back," said an American who had not yet spoken. " 'Wonder if our forebears knew how she was going to grow."

" A very large country." The speaker sighed as though the weight of it from New York to 'Frisco lay upon his shoulders. " If ever we do divide, it means that we are done for. There is no room for four first-class empires in the States. One split will lead to another if the first is successful. What's the use of talking ? "

What was the use ? Here's our conversation as it ran, the night of the Queen's Birthday. What do *you* think ?

II.

"Serene, indifferent to fate,
Thou sittest at the western gate,
Thou seest the white seas fold their tents,
Oh warder of two Continents.
Thou drawest all things small and great
To thee beside the Western Gate."

THIS is what Bret Harte has written of the
great city of San Francisco, and for the past
fortnight I have been wondering what made
him do it.

There is neither serenity nor indifference
to be found in these parts ; and evil would it
be for the Continent whose wardship were intrusted to so reckless a guardian.

Behold me pitched neck-and-crop from
twenty days of the High Seas, into the whirl
of California, deprived of any guidance, and
left to draw my own conclusions. Protect me
from the wrath of an outraged community if
these letters be ever read by American eyes.
San Francisco is a mad city—inhabited for
the most part by perfectly insane people
whose women are of a remarkable beauty.

When the *City of Peking* steamed through
the Golden Gate I saw with great joy that the
block-house which guarded the mouth of the
" finest harbor in the world, Sir," could be

silenced by two gunboats from Hong-Kong with safety, comfort, and despatch.

Then a reporter leaped aboard, and ere I could gasp held me in his toils. He pumped me exhaustively while I was getting ashore, demanding, of all things in the world, news about Indian journalism. It is an awful thing to enter a new land with a new lie on your lips. I spoke the truth to the evil-minded Custom-house man who turned my most sacred raiment on a floor composed of stable-refuse and pine-splinters; but the reporter overwhelmed me not so much by his poignant audacity as his beautiful ignorance. I am sorry now that I did not tell him more lies as I passed into a city of three hundred thousand white men. Think of it! Three hundred thousand white men and women gathered in one spot, walking upon real pavements in front of real plate-glass windowed shops, and talking something that was not very different from English. It was only when I had tangled myself up in a hopeless maze of small wooden houses, dust, street-refuse, and children who play with empty kerosene tins, that I discovered the difference of speech.

"You want to go to the Palace Hotel?" said an affable youth on a dray. "What in hell are you doing here, then? This is about the lowest place in the city. Go six blocks north to the corner of Geary and Market; then walk around till you strike corner of

Gutter and Sixteenth, and that brings you there."

I do not vouch for the literal accuracy of these directions, quoting but from a disordered memory.

"Amen," I said. "But who am I that I should strike the corners of such as you name? Peradventure they be gentlemen of repute, and might hit back. Bring it down to dots, my son."

I thought he would have smitten me, but he didn't. He explained that no one ever used the word "street," and that every one was supposed to know how the streets run: for sometimes the names were upon the lamps and sometimes they weren't. Fortified with these directions I proceeded till I found a mighty street full of sumptuous buildings four or five stories high, but paved with rude cobble-stones in the fashion of the Year One. A cable-car without any visible means of support slid stealthily behind me and nearly struck me in the back. A hundred yards further there was a slight commotion in the street—a gathering together of three or four —and something glittered as it moved very swiftly. A ponderous Irish gentleman with priest's cords in his hat and a small nickel-plated badge on his fat bosom emerged from the knot, supporting a Chinaman who had been stabbed in the eye and was bleeding like a pig. The bystanders went their ways, and the Chinaman, assisted by the policeman, his own. Of course this was none of my business, but I rather wanted to know what had happened to the gentleman who had dealt the stab. It said a great deal for the excellence of the municipal arrangements of the town that a surging crowd did not at once block the street to see what was going forward. I was the sixth man and the last who assisted at the performance, and my curiosity was six times the greatest. Indeed, I felt ashamed of showing it.

There were no more incidents till I reached the Palace Hotel, a seven-storied warren of humanity with a thousand rooms in it. All the travel-books will tell you about hotel arrangements in this country. They should be seen to be appreciated. Understand clearly—and this letter is written after a thousand miles of experiences—that money will not buy you service in the West.

When the hotel clerk—the man who awards your room to you and who is supposed to give you information—when that resplendent individual stoops to attend to your wants, he does so whistling or humming, or picking his teeth, or pauses to converse with some one he knows. These performances, I gather, are to impress upon you that he is a free man and your equal. From his general appearance and the size of his diamonds he ought to be your superior. There is no necessity for this swaggering self-consciousness of freedom, Business is business, and the man who is paid to attend to a man might reasonably devote his whole attention to the job.

In a vast marble-paved hall under the glare of an electric light sat forty or fifty men; and for their use and amusement were provided spittoons of infinite capacity and generous gape. Most of the men wore frock-coats and top-hats,—the things that we in India put on at a wedding breakfast if we possessed them, —but they all spat. They spat on principle. The spittoons were on the staircases, in each bedroom—yea, and in chambers even more sacred than these. They chased one into retirement, but they blossomed in chiefest splendor round the Bar, and they were all used, every reeking one of 'em.

Just before I began to feel deathly sick, another reporter grappled me. What he wanted to know was the precise area of India in square miles. I referred him to Whittaker. He had never heard of Whittaker. He wanted it from my own mouth, and I would not tell him. Then he swerved off, like the other man, to details of journalism in our own country. I ventured to suggest that the interior economy of a paper most concerned the people who worked it. "That's the very thing that interests us," he said. "Have you got reporters anything like our reporters on Indian newspapers?" "We have not," I said, and suppressed the " thank God " rising to my lips. " *Why* haven't you ? " said he. " Because they would die," I said. It was exactly like talking to a child—a very rude little child. He would begin almost every sentence with : " Now tell me something about India," and would turn aimlessly from one question to another without the least continuity. I was not angry, but keenly interested. The man was a revelation to me. To his questions I returned answers mendacious and evasive. After all, it really did not matter what I said. He could not understand. I can only hope and pray that none of the readers of the *Pioneer* will ever see that portentous interview. The man made me out to be an idiot several sizes more driveling than my destiny intended, and the rankness of his ignorance managed to distort the few poor facts with which I supplied him into large and elaborate lies. Then thought I : " The matter of American journalism shall be looked into later on. At present I will enjoy myself."

No man rose to tell me what were the lions of the place. No one volunteered any sort of conveyance. I was absolutely alone in this big city of white folk. By instinct I sought refreshment and came upon a bar-room, full of bad Salon pictures, in which men with hats on the backs of their heads were wolfing food from a counter. It was the institution of the " Free Lunch " that I had struck. You paid

for a drink and got as much as you wanted to
eat.   For something less than a rupee a day
a man can feed himself sumptuously in San
Francisco, even though he be bankrupt.   Remember this if ever you are stranded in these
parts.

Later, I began a vast but unsystematic exploration of the streets.   I asked for no names.
It was enough that the pavements were full of
white men and women, the streets clanging
with traffic, and that the restful roar of a great
city rang in my ears.   The cable-cars glided
to all points of the compass.   I took them
one by one till I could go no farther.   San
Francisco has been pitched down on the sand
bunkers of the Bikaneer desert.   About one-
fourth of it is ground reclaimed from the sea
—any old-timer will tell you all about that.
The remainder is ragged, unthrifty sand-hills,
pegged down by houses.

From an English point of view there has
not been the least attempt at grading those
hills, and indeed you might as well try to grade
the hillocks of Sind.   The cable-cars have for
all practical purposes made San Francisco a
dead level.   They take no count of rise or fall,
but slide equably on their appointed courses
from one end to the other of a six-mile street.
They turn corners almost at right angles; cross
other lines, and, for aught I know, may run
up the sides of houses.   There is no visible
agency of their flight; but once in a while

you shall pass a five-storied building, humming
with machinery that winds up an everlasting
wire-cable, and the initiated will tell you that
here is the mechanism. I gave up asking
questions. If it pleases Providence to make a
car run up and down a slit in the ground for
many miles, and if for twopence-halfpenny I
can ride in that car, why shall I seek the reasons of the miracle? Rather let me look out
of the windows till the shops give place to
thousands and thousands of little houses made
of wood—each house just big enough for a
man and his family. Let me watch the people in the cars, and try to find out in what
manner they differ from us, their ancestors.

They delude themselves into the belief that
they talk English,—*the* English,—and I have
already been pitied for speaking with "an
English accent." The man who pitied me
spoke, so far as I was concerned, the language
of thieves. And they all do. Where we put
the accent forward, they throw it back, and
vice versa ; where we use the long *a*, they use
the short ; and words so simple as to be past
mistaking, they pronounce somewhere up in
the dome of their heads. How do these things
happen?

Oliver Wendell Holmes says that Yankee
schoolmarms, the cider, and the salt codfish
of the Eastern States are responsible for what
he calls a nasal accent. A Hindu is a Hindu,
and a brother to the man who knows his ver-

nacular; and a Frenchman is French because
he speaks his own language; but the American has no language. He is dialect, slang,
provincialism, accent, and so forth. Now that
I have heard their voices, all the beauty of
Bret Harte is being ruined for me, because I
find myself catching through the roll of his
rhythmical prose the cadence of his peculiar
fatherland. Get an American lady to read to
you " How Santa Claus came to Simpson's
Bar," and see how much is, under her tongue,
left of the beauty of the original.

But I am sorry for Bret Harte. It happened this way. A reporter asked me what I
thought of the city, and I made answer suavely
that it was hallowed ground to me because of
Bret Harte. That was true.

"Well," said the reporter, " Bret Harte
claims California, but California don't claim
Bret Harte. He's been so long in England
that he's quite English. Have you seen our
cracker-factories and the new offices of the
Examiner? " He could not understand that
to the outside world the city was worth a great
deal less than the man.

*   *   *   *   *

Night fell over the Pacific, and the white
sea-fog whipped through the streets, dimming
the splendors of the electric lights. It is the
use of this city, her men and women, to parade
between the hours of eight and ten a certain

street, called Kearney Street, where the finest
shops are situated. Here the click of heels
on the pavement is loudest, here the lights are
brightest, and here the thunder of the traffic is
most overwhelming. I watched Young California and saw that it was at least expensively
dressed, cheerful in manner, and self-asserting
in conversation. Also the women are very
fair. The maidens were of generous build,
large, well-groomed, and attired in raiment
that even to my inexperienced eyes must have
cost much. Kearney Street, at nine o'clock,
levels all distinctions of rank as impartially as
the grave. Again and again I loitered at the
heels of a couple of resplendent beings, only
to overhear, when I expected the level voice
of culture, the *staccato* " Sez he," " Sez I,"
that is the mark of the white servant-girl all
the world over.

This was depressing because, in spite of all
that goes to the contrary, fine feathers ought
to make fine birds. There was wealth—unlimited wealth—in the streets, but not an accent that would not have been dear at fifty
cents. Wherefore, revolving in my mind that
these folk were barbarians, I was presently enlightened and made aware that they also were
the heirs of all the ages, and civilized after all.
There appeared before me an affable stranger
of prepossessing appearance, with a blue and
an innocent eye. Addressing me by name,
he claimed to have met me in New York at

the Windsor, and to this claim I gave a quali-
fied assent. I did not remember the fact, but
since he was so certain of it, why then—I
waited developments.

"And what did you think of Indiana when
you came through?" was the next question.

It revealed the mystery of previous acquaintance, and one or two other things.
With reprehensible carelessness, my friend of
the light-blue eye had looked up the name
of his victim in the hotel register and read
" India " for Indiana.

He could not imagine an Englishman coming through the States from West to East instead of by the regularly ordained route. My
fear was that in his delight at finding me so
responsive he would make remarks about New
York and the Windsor which I could not
understand. And indeed, he adventured in
this direction once or twice, asking me what I
thought of such and such streets, which, from
his tone, I gathered were anything but respectable. It is trying to talk unknown New
York in almost unknown San Francisco. But
my friend was merciful. He protested that I
was one after his own heart, and pressed upon
me rare and curious drinks at more than one
bar. These drinks I accepted with gratitude,
as also the cigars with which his pockets were
stored. He would show me the Life of the
city. Having no desire to watch a weary old
play again, I evaded the offer, and received in

lieu of the Devil's instruction much coarse flattery. Curiously constituted is the soul of man. Knowing how and where this man lied; waiting idly for the finale; I was distinctly conscious, as he bubbled compliments in my ear, of soft thrills of gratified pride. I was wise, quoth he, anybody could see that with half an eye; sagacious; versed in the affairs of the world; an acquaintance to be desired; one who had tasted the cup of Life with discretion.

All this pleased me, and in a measure numbed the suspicion that was thoroughly aroused Eventually the blue-eyed one discovered, nay insisted, that I had a taste for cards (this was clumsily worked in, but it was my fault, in that I met him half-way, and allowed him no chance of good acting). Hereupon, I laid my head to one side, and simulated unholy wisdom, quoting odds and ends of poker-talk, all ludicrously misapplied. My friend kept his countenance admirably; and well he might, for five minutes later we arrived, always by the purest of chances, at a place where we could play cards, and also frivol with Louisiana State Lottery tickets. Would I play?

"Nay," said I, "for to me cards have neither meaning nor continuity; but let us assume that I am going to play. How would you and your friends get to work? Would you play a straight game or make me drunk,

3

or—well, the fact is I'm a newspaper man, and I'd be much obliged if you'd let me know something about bunco-steering."

My blue-eyed friend cursed me by his gods, —the Right and the Left Bower ; he even cursed the very good cigars he had given me. But, the storm over, he quieted down and ex- plained. I apologized for causing him to waste an evening, and we spent a very pleasant time together.

Inaccuracy, provincialism, and a too hasty rushing to conclusions were the rocks that he had split on ; but he got his revenge when he said :

" How would I play with you ? From all the poppycock " (*Anglice*, bosh) " you talked about poker, I'd ha' played a straight game and skinned you. I wouldn't have taken the trouble to make you drunk. You never knew anything of the game ; but the way I was mistaken in you makes me sick."

He glared at me as though I had done him an injury. To-day I know how it is that, year after year, week after week, the bunco-steerer, who is the confidence-trick and the card-sharper man of other climes, secures his prey. He slavers them over with flattery, as the snake slavers the rabbit. The incident depressed me because it showed I had left the innocent East far behind, and was come to a country where a man must look out for himself. The very hotel glistened with notices about keep-

ing my door locked, and depositing my valu-
ables in a safe. The white man in a lump is
bad. Weeping softly for O-Toyo (little I
knew then that my heart was to be torn
afresh from my bosom!), I fell asleep in the
clanging hotel.

Next morning I had entered upon the De-
ferred Inheritance. There are no princes in
America,—at least with crowns on their heads,
—but a generous-minded member of some
royal family received my letter of introduction. Ere the day closed I was a member of
the two clubs and booked for many engage-
ments to dinner and party. Now this prince,
upon whose financial operations be continual
increase, had no reason, nor had the others, his
friends, to put himself out for the sake of one
Briton more or less ; but he rested not till he
had accomplished all in my behalf that a
mother could think of for her *débutante* daughter. Do you know the Bohemian Club of San
Francisco ? They say its fame extends over
the world. It was created somewhat on the
lines of the Savage by men who wrote or drew
things, and it has blossomed into most unre-
publican luxury. The ruler of the place is an
owl—an owl standing upon a skull and cross-
bones, showing forth grimly the wisdom of the
man of letters and the end of his hopes for
immortality. The owl stands on the stair-
case, a statue four feet high, is carved in the
woodwork, flutters on the frescoed ceilings, is

stamped on the note-paper, and hangs on the walls. He is an Ancient and Honorable Bird. Under his wing 'twas my privilege to meet with white men whose lives were not chained down to routine of toil, who wrote magazine articles instead of reading them hurriedly in the pauses of office-work, who painted pictures instead of contenting themselves with cheap etchings picked up at another man's sale of effects. Mine were all the rights of social intercourse that India, stony-hearted stepmother of Collectors, has swindled us out of. Treading soft carpets and breathing the incense of superior cigars, I wandered from room to room studying the paintings in which the members of the club had caricatured themselves, their associates, and their aims. There was a slick French audacity about the workmanship of these men of toil unbending that went straight to the heart of the beholder. And yet it was not altogether French. A dry grimness of treatment, almost Dutch, marked the difference. The men painted as they spoke—with certainty. The club indulges in revelries which it calls " jinks "—high and low,—at intervals,—and each of these gatherings is faithfully portrayed in oils by hands that know their business. In this club were no amateurs spoiling canvas because they fancied they could handle oils without knowledge of shadows or anatomy—no gentleman of leisure ruining the temper of publishers and

an already ruined market with attempts to
write "because everybody writes something
these days."

My hosts were working, or had worked, for
their daily bread with pen or paint, and their
talk for the most part was of the shop shoppy
—-that is to say, delightful.   They extended a
large hand of welcome and were as brethren,
and I did homage to the Owl and listened to
their talk.   An Indian Club about Christmas-
time will yield, if properly worked, an abun-
dant harvest of queer tales ; but at a gathering
of Americans from the uttermost ends of their
own continent the tales are largeɪ, thicker,
more spinous, and even more azure than any
Indian variety.   Tales of the War I heard
told by an ex-officer of the South over his
evening drink to a Colonel of the Northern
army ; my introducer, who had served as a
trooper in the Northern Horse, throwing in
emendations from time to time.

Other voices followed with equally wondrous tales of riata-throwing in Mexico or
Arizona, of gambling at army posts in Texas,
of newspaper wars waged in godless Chicago,
of deaths sudden and violent in Montana. and
Dakota, of the loves of half-breed maidens in
the South, and fantastic huntings for gold in
mysterious Alaska.   Above all, they told the
story of the building of old San Francisco,
when the " finest collection of humanity on
God's earth, Sir, started this town, and the

water came up to the foot of Market Street."
Very terrible were some of the tales, grimly
humorous the others, and the men in broad-
cloth and fine linen who told them had played
their parts in them.

" And now and again when things got too
bad they would toll the city bell, and the
Vigilance Committee turned out and hanged
the suspicious characters. A man didn't
begin to be suspected in those days till he had
committed at least one unprovoked murder,"
said a calm-eyed, portly old gentleman.

I looked at the pictures around me, the
noiseless, neat-uniformed waiter behind me,
the oak-ribbed ceiling above, the velvety carpet beneath. It was hard to realize that even
twenty years ago you could see a man hanged
with great pomp. Later on I found reason to
change my opinion. The tales gave me a
headache and set me thinking. How in the
world was it possible to take in even one-
thousandth of this huge, roaring, many-sided
continent ? In the silence of the sumptuous
library lay Professor Bryce's book on the
American Republic.

" It is an omen," said I. " He has done
all things in all seriousness, and he may be
purchased for half a guinea. Those who
desire information of the most undoubted
must refer to his pages. For me is the daily
round of vagabondage, the recording of the
incidents of the hour, and talk with the trav-

eling companion of the day. I will not 'do' this country at all."

And I forgot all about India for ten days while I went out to dinners and watched the social customs of the people, which are entirely different from our customs, and was introduced to the men of many millions. These persons are harmless in their earlier stages ; that is to say, a man worth three or four million dollars may be a good talker, clever, amusing, and of the world ; a man with twice that amount is to be avoided ; and a twenty-million man is— just twenty millions. Take an instance. I was speaking to a newspaper man about seeing the proprietor of his journal. My friend snorted indignantly :

" See *him !* Great Scott ! *No !* If he happens to appear in the office, I have to associate with him ; but, thank Heaven, outside of that I move in circles where he cannot come."

And yet the first thing I have been taught to believe is that money was everything in America !

III.

" Poor men—God made, and all for that ! "

IT was a bad business throughout, and the only consolation is that it was all my fault.

A man took me round the Chinese quarter of San Francisco, which is a ward of the city of Canton set down in the most eligible business-quarter of the place.

The Chinaman with his usual skill has possessed himself of good brick fire-proof buildings and, following instinct, has packed each tenement with hundreds of souls, all living in filth and squalor not to be appreciated save by you in India. That cursory investigation ought to have sufficed ; but I wanted to know how deep in the earth the Pig-tail had taken root. Therefore I explore the Chinese quarter a second time and alone, which was foolishness. No one in the filthy streets (but for the blessed sea breezes San Francisco would enjoy cholera every season) interfered with my movements, though many asked for *cumshaw*. I struck a house about four stories high full of celestial abominations, and began to burrow down ; having heard that these tenements were constructed on the lines of icebergs—two-thirds below sight level. Down-

stairs I crawled past Chinamen in bunks,
opium-smokers, brothels, and gambling hells,
till I had reached the second cellar—was, in
fact, in the labyrinths of a warren. Great is
the wisdom of the Chinaman. In time of
trouble that house could be razed to the
ground by the mob, and yet hide all its inhabitants in brick-walled and wooden-beamed
subterranean galleries, strengthened with iron-
framed doors and gates. On the second
underground floor a man asked for *cumshaw*
and took me down-stairs to yet another cellar,
where the air was as thick as butter, and the
lamps burned little holes in it not more than
an inch square. In this place a poker club
had assembled and was in full swing. The
Chinaman loves " pokel," and plays it with
great skill, swearing like a cat when he loses.
Most of the men round the table were in semi-
European dress, their pig-tails curled up under
billy-cock hats. One of the company looked
like a Eurasian, whence I argued that he was
a Mexican—a supposition that later inquiries
confirmed. They were a picturesque set of
fiends and polite, being too absorbed in their
game to look at the stranger. We were all
deep down under the earth, and save for the
rustle of a blue gown sleeve and the ghostly
whisper of the cards as they were shuffled
and played, there was no sound. The heat
was almost unendurable. There was some
dispute between the Mexican and the man on

his left. The latter shifted his place to put the table between himself and his opponent, and stretched a lean yellow hand towards the Mexican's winnings.

Mark how purely man is a creature of instinct. Rarely introduced to the pistol, I saw the Mexican half rise in his chair and at the same instant found myself full length on the floor. None had told me that this was the best attitude when bullets are abroad. I was there prone before I had time to think—dropping as the room was filled with an intolerable clamor like the discharge of a cannon. In those close quarters the pistol report had no room to spread any more than the smoke—then acrid in my nostrils. There was no second shot, but a great silence in which I rose slowly to my knees. The Chinaman was gripping the table with both hands and staring in front of him at an empty chair. The Mexican had gone, and a little whirl of smoke was floating near the roof. Still gripping the table, the Chinaman said: " Ah ! " in the tone that a man would use when, looking up from his work suddenly, he sees a well-known friend in the doorway. Then he coughed and fell over to his own right, and I saw that he had been shot in the stomach.

I became aware that, save for two men leaning over the stricken one, the room was empty ; and all the tides of intense fear, hitherto held back by intenser curiosity, swept over my soul. I ardently desired the outside air. It was possible that the Chinamen would mistake me for the Mexican,—everything horrible seemed possible just then,—and it was more than possible that the stairways would be closed while they were hunting for the murderer. The man on the floor coughed a sickening cough. I heard it as I fled, and one of his companions turned out the lamp. Those stairs seemed interminable, and to add to my dismay there was no sound of commotion in the house. No one hindered, no one even looked at me. There was no trace of the Mexican. I found the doorway and, my legs trembling under me, reached the protection of the clear cool night, the fog, and the rain. I dared not run, and for the life of me I could not walk. I must have effected a compromise, for I remember the light of a street lamp showed the shadow of one half skipping—caracoling along the pavements in what seemed to be an ecstasy of suppressed happiness. But it was fear—deadly fear. Fear compounded of past knowledge of the Oriental—only other white man—available witness—three stories underground—and the cough of the Chinaman now some forty feet under my clattering boot-heels. It was good to see the shop-fronts and electric lights again. Not for anything would I have informed the police, because I firmly believed that the Mexican had been dealt with somewhere down there on the third floor long ere I had reached the air ; and, moreover, once clear of the place, I could not for the life of me tell where it was.   My ill-considered flight brought me out somewhere a mile distant from the hotel ; and the clank of the lift that bore me to a bed six stories above ground was music in my ears.   Wherefore I would impress it upon you who follow after, do not knock about the Chinese quarters at night and alone.   You may stumble across a picturesque piece of human nature that will unsteady your nerves for half a day.

      *   *   *   *   *

And this brings me by natural sequence to the great drink question.   As you know, of course, the American does not drink at meals as a sensible man should.   Indeed, he has no meals.   He stuffs for ten minutes thrice a day. Also he has no decent notions about the sun being over the yard-arm or below the horizon. He pours his vanity into himself at unholy hours, and indeed he can hardly help it.   You have no notion of what " treating " means on the Western slope.   It is more than an insti-tution ; it is a religion, though men tell me that it is nothing to what it was.   Take a very com-mon instance.   At 10.30 A. M. a man is smit-ten with a desire for stimulants.   He is in the company of two friends.   All three ad-journ to the nearest bar,—seldom more than twenty yards away,—and take three straight whiskies. They talk for two minutes. The second and third man then treats in order ; and thus each walks into the street, two of them the poorer by three goes of whisky under their belt and one with two more liquors than he wanted. It is not etiquette yet to refuse a treat. The result is peculiar. I have never yet, I confess, seen a drunken man in the streets, but I have heard more about drunkenness among white men, and seen more decent men above or below themselves with drink, than I care to think about. And the vice runs up into all sorts of circles and societies. Never was I more astonished than at one pleasant dinner party to hear a pair of pretty lips say casually of a gentleman friend then under discussion, " He was drunk." The fact was merely stated without emotion. That was what startled me. But the climate of California deals kindly with excess, and treacherously covers up its traces. A man neither bloats nor shrivels in this dry air. He continues with the false bloom of health upon his cheeks, an equable eye, a firm mouth, and a steady hand till a day of reckoning arrives, and suddenly breaking up, about the head, he dies, and his friends speak his epitaph accordingly. Why people who in most cases cannot hold their liquor should play with it so recklessly I leave to others to decide. This unhappy state of affairs has, however, produced one good result which I will confide to you. In the heart of the business quarter, where banks and bankers are thickest, and telegraph wires most numerous, stands a semi-subterranean bar tended by a German with long blond locks and a crystalline eye. Go thither softly, treading on the tips of your toes, and ask him for a Button Punch. 'Twill take ten minutes to brew, but the result is the highest and noblest product of the age. No man but one knows what is in it. I have a theory it is compounded of the shavings of cherubs' wings, the glory of a tropical dawn, the red clouds of sunset, and fragments of lost epics by dead masters. But try you for yourselves, and pause a while to bless me, who am always mindful of the truest interests of my brethren.

But enough of the stale spilth of bar-rooms. Turn now to the august spectacle of a Government of the people, by the people, for the people, as it is understood in the city of San Francisco. Professor Bryce's book will tell you that every American citizen over twenty-one years of age possesses a vote. He may not know how to run his own business, control his wife, or instil reverence into his children, may be pauper, half-crazed with drink, bankrupt, dissolute, or merely a born fool; but he has a vote. If he likes, he can be voting most of his time—voting for his State Governor, his municipal officers, local option,

sewage contracts, or anything else of which
he has no special knowledge.

Once every four years he votes for a new
President. In his spare moments he votes
for his own judges—the men who shall
give him justice. These are dependent on
popular favor for re-election inasmuch as they
are but chosen for a term of years—two or
three, I believe. Such a position is mani-
festly best calculated to create an independent and unprejudiced administrator. Now
this mass of persons who vote is divided into
two parties—Republican and Democrat. They
are both agreed in thinking that the other
part is running creation (which is America)
into red flame. Also the Democrat as a party
drinks more than the Republican, and when
drunk may be heard to talk about a thing
called the Tariff, which he does not understand, but which he conceives to be the bul-
wark of the country or else the surest power
for its destruction. Sometimes he says one
thing and sometimes another, in order to
contradict the Republican, who is always con-
tradicting himself. And this is a true and
lucid account of the forepart of American
politics. The behind-part is otherwise.

Since every man has a vote and may vote
on every conceivable thing, it follows that
there exist certain wise men who understand
the art of buying up votes retail, and vending
them wholesale to whoever wants them most

urgently. Now an American engaged in making a home for himself has not time to vote for turncocks and district attorneys and cattle of that kind, but the unemployed have much time because they are always on hand somewhere in the streets. They are called " the boys," and form a peculiar class. The boys are young men; inexpert in war, unskilled in labor; who have neither killed a man, lifted cattle, or dug a well. In plain English, they are just the men in the streets who can always be trusted to rally round any cause that has a glass of liquor for a visible heart. They wait—they are on hand—; and in being on hand lies the crown and the glory of American politics. The wise man is he who, keeping a liquor saloon and judiciously dispensing drinks, knows how to retain within arm's reach a block of men who will vote for or against anything under the canopy of Heaven. Not every saloon-keeper can do this. It demands careful study of city politics, tact, the power of conciliation, and infinite resources of anecdote to amuse and keep the crowd together night after night, till the saloon becomes a salon. Above all, the liquor side of the scheme must not be worked for immediate profit. The boys who drink so freely will ultimately pay their host a thousandfold. An Irishman, and an Irishman pre-eminently, knows how to work such a saloon parliament. Observe for a moment

the plan of operations. The rank and file
are treated to drink and a little money—and
they vote. He who controls ten votes re-
ceives a proportionate reward; the dispenser
of a thousand votes is worthy of reverence,
and so the chain runs on till we reach the
most successful worker of public saloons—the
man most skilful in keeping his items together and using them when required. Such
a man governs the city as absolutely as a
king. And you would know where the gain
comes in? The whole of the public offices of
a city (with the exception of a very few where
special technical skill is required) are short-term
offices distributed according to "political" lean-
ings. What would you have? A big city requires many officials. Each office carries a sal-
ary and influence worth twice the pay. The
offices are for the representatives of the men
who keep together and are on hand to vote.
The Commissioner of Sewage, let us say, is a
gentleman who has been elected to his office by
a Republican vote. He knows little and cares
less about sewage, but he has sense enough
to man the pumping-works and the street-
sweeping - machines with the gentlemen
who elected him. The Commissioner of
Police has been helped to his post very
largely by the influence of the boys at such
and such a saloon. He may be the guardian
of city morals, but he is not going to allow
his subordinates to enforce early closing or

4

abstention from gambling in that saloon.
Most offices are limited to four years, consequently he is a fool who does not make his
office pay him while he is in it.

The only people who suffer by this happy
arrangement are, in fact, the people who de-
vised the lovely system. And they suffer
because they are Americans. Let us explain.
As you know, every big city here holds at
least one big foreign vote—generally Irish,
frequently German. In San Francisco, the
gathering place of the races, there is a distinct
Italian vote to be considered, but the Irish
vote is more important. For this reason the
Irishman does not kill himself with overwork.
He is made for the cheery dispensing of
liquors, for everlasting blarney, and possesses
a wonderfully keen appreciation of the weak-
nesses of lesser human nature. Also he has
no sort of conscience, and only one strong
conviction—that of deep-rooted hatred toward
England. He keeps to the streets, he is on
hand, he votes joyously, spending days lavishly,—and time is the American's dearest com-
modity. Behold the glorious result. To-day
the city of San Francisco is governed by the
Irish vote and the Irish influence, under the
rule of a gentleman whose sight is impaired,
and who requires a man to lead him about the
streets. He is called officially " Boss Buckley," and unofficially the " Blind White Devil."
I have before me now the record of his

amiable career in black and white.   It occupies
four columns of small print, and perhaps you
would think it disgraceful.   Summarized, it is
as follows : Boss Buckley, by tact and deep
knowledge of the seamy side of the city, won
himself a following of voters.   He sought no
office himself, or rarely : but as his following
increased he sold their services to the highest
bidder, himself taking toll of the revenues of
every office.   He controlled the Democratic
party in the city of San Francisco.   The
people appoint their own judges.   Boss Buckley's people appointed judges.   These judges
naturally were Boss Buckley's property.   I
have been to dinner parties and heard educated men, not concerned with politics, telling
stories one to another of " justice," both civil
and criminal, being bought with a price from
the hands of these judges.   Such tales they
told without heat, as men recording facts.
Contracts for road-mending, public buildings,
and the like are under the control of Boss
Buckley, because the men whom Buckley's
following sent to the City Council adjudicate
on these contracts ; and on each and every one
of these contracts Boss Buckley levies his
percentage for himself and his allies.

The Republican party in San Francisco also
have their boss.   He is not so great a genius
as Boss Buckley, but I decline to believe that
he is any whit more virtuous.   He has a
smaller number of votes at his command.

IV.

I HAVE been watching machinery in repose after reading about machinery in action.

An excellent gentleman who bears a name honored in the magazines writes, much as Disraeli orated, of " the sublime instincts of an ancient people," the certainty with which they can be trusted to manage their own affairs in their own way, and the speed with which they are making for all sorts of desirable goals. This he called a statement or purview of American politics.

I went almost directly afterwards to a saloon where gentlemen interested in ward politics nightly congregate. They were not pretty persons. Some of them were bloated, and they all swore cheerfully till the heavy gold watch-chains on their fat stomachs rose and fell again ; but they talked over their liquor as men who had power and unquestioned access to places of trust and profit.

The magazine-writer discussed theories of government ; these men the practice. They had been there. They knew all about it. They banged their fist on the table and spoke of political " pulls," the vending of votes, and so forth. Theirs was not the talk of village babblers reconstructing the affairs of the na-

tion, but of strong, coarse, lustful men fighting
for spoil and thoroughly understanding the
best methods of reaching it.   I listened long
and intently to speech I could not understand,
or only in spots.   It was the speech of business, however.   I had sense enough to know
that, and to do my laughing outside the door.
Then I began to understand why my pleasant
and well-educated hosts in San Francisco
spoke with a bitter scorn of such duties of
citizenship as voting and taking an interest in
the distribution of offices.   Scores of men
have told me with no false pride that they
would as soon concern themselves with the
public affairs of the city or State as rake
muck.   Read about politics as the cultured
writer of the magazines regards 'em, and then,
and not till then, pay your respects to the
gentlemen who run the grimy reality.

I'm sick of interviewing night-editors, who,
in response to my demand for the record of a
prominent citizen, answers : " Well, you see, he
began by keeping a saloon," etc.   I prefer to
believe that my informants are treating me as
in the old sinful days in India I was used to
treat our wandering Globe-trotters.   They
declare that they speak the truth, and the
news of dog-politics lately vouchsafed to me in
groggeries incline me to believe—but I won't.
The people are much too nice to slangander
as recklessly as I have been doing.   Besides,
I am hopelessly in love with about eight

American maidens—all perfectly delightful till the next one comes into the room. O-Toyo was a darling, but she lacked several things ; conversation, for one. You cannot live on giggles. She shall remain unmoved at Nagasaki while I roast a battered heart before the shrine of a big Kentucky blonde who had for a nurse, when she was little, a negro "mammy." By consequence she has welded on to Californian beauty, Paris dresses, Eastern culture, Europe trips, and wild Western originality, the queer dreamy superstitions of the negro quarters, and the result is soul-shattering. And she is but one of many stars. *Item*, a maiden who believes in education and possesses it, with a few hundred thousand dollars to boot, and a taste for slumming. *Item*, the leader of a sort of informal salon where girls congregate, read papers, and daringly discuss metaphysical problems and candy—a sloe-eyed, black-browed imperious maiden. *Item*, a very small maiden, absolutely without reverence, who can in one swift sentence trample upon and leave gasping half a dozen young men. *Item*, a millionairess, burdened with her money, lonely, caustic, with a tongue keen as a sword, yearning for a sphere, but chained up to the rock of her vast possessions. *Item*, a type-writer-maiden earning her own bread in this big city, because she doesn't think a girl ought to be a burden on her parents. She quotes

Théophile Gautier, and moves through the world manfully, much respected, for all her twenty inexperienced summers. *Item*, a woman from Cloudland who has no history in the past, but is discreetly of the present, and strives for the confidences of male humanity on the grounds of " sympathy." (This is not altogether a new type.) *Item*, a girl in a " dive " blessed with a Greek head and eyes that seem to speak all that is best and sweetest in the world. But wo is me !—she has no ideas in this world or the next, beyond the consumption of beer (a commission on each bottle), and protests that she sings the songs allotted to her nightly with no more than the vaguest notion of their meaning.

Sweet and comely are the maidens of Devonshire; delicate and of gracious seeming those who live in the pleasant places of London ; fascinating for all their demureness the damsels of France clinging closely to their mothers, and with large eyes wondering at the wicked world; excellent in her own place and to those who understand her is the Anglo-Indian " spin " in her second season ; but the girls of America are above and beyond them all. They are clever; they can talk. Yea, it is said that they think. Certainly they have an appearance of so doing. They are original, and look you between the brows with unabashed eyes as a sister might look at her brother. They are instructed in the folly and

vanity of the male mind, for they have associated with "the boys" from babyhood, and can
discerningly minister to both vices, or pleasantly snub the possessor. They possess,
moreover, a life among themselves, independent of masculine associations. They have
societies and clubs and unlimited tea-fights
where all the guests are girls. They are self-
possessed without parting with any tenderness
that is their sex-right ; they understand ; they
can take care of themselves ; they are superbly
independent. When you ask them what
makes them so charming, they say : " It is because we are better educated than your girls
and—and we are more sensible in regard to
men. We have good times all around, but
we aren't taught to regard every man as a
possible husband. Nor is he expected to
marry the first girl he calls on regularly." Yes,
they have good times, their freedom is large,
and they do not abuse it. They can go driving with young men, and receive visits from
young men to an extent that would make an
English mother wink with horror ; and neither
driver nor drivee have a thought beyond the
enjoyment of a good time. As certain also of
their own poets have said :—

" Man is fire and woman is tow,
And the devil he comes and begins to blow."

In America the tow is soaked in a solution
that makes it fireproof, in absolute liberty

and large knowledge: consequently accidents do not exceed the regular percentage arranged by the Devil for each class and climate under the skies. But the freedom of the young girl has its drawbacks. She is—I say it with all reluctance—irreverent, from her forty-dollar bonnet to the buckles in her eighteen-dollar shoes. She talks flippantly to her parents and men old enough to be her grandfather. She has a prescriptive right to the society of the Man who Arrives. The parents admit it. This is sometimes embarrassing, especially when you call on a man and his wife for the sake of information ; the one being a merchant of varied knowledge, the other a woman of the world. In five minutes your host has vanished. In another five his wife has followed him, and you are left with a very charming maiden doubtless, but certainly not the person you came to see. She chatters and you grin ; but you leave with the very strong impression of a wasted morning. This has been my experience once or twice. I have even said as pointedly as I dared to a man : " I came to see you." " You'd better see me in my office, then. The house belongs to my women-folk—to my daughter, that is to say." He spoke with truth. The American of wealth is owned by his family. They exploit him for bullion, and sometimes it seems to me that his lot is a lonely one. The women get the ha'pence ; the kicks are all his own.

Nothing is too good for an American's daughter (I speak here of the moneyed classes). The girls take every gift as a matter of course. Yet they develop greatly when a catastrophe arrives and the man of many millions goes up or goes down and his daughters take to stenography or typewriting. I have heard many tales of heroism from the lips of girls who counted the principals among their friends. The crash came; Mamie or Hattie or Sadie gave up their maid, their carriages and candy, and with a No. 2 Remington and a stout heart set about earning their daily bread.

"And did I drop her from the list of my friends? No, sir," said a scarlet-lipped vision in white lace. "That might happen to me any day."

It may be this sense of possible disaster in the air that makes San Franciscan society go with so captivating a rush and whirl. Recklessness is in the air. I can't explain where it comes from, but there it is. The roaring winds off the Pacific make you drunk to begin with. The aggressive luxury on all sides helps out the intoxication, and you spin for ever " down the ringing groves of change " (there is no small change, by the way, west of the Rockies) as long as money lasts. They make greatly and they spend lavishly ; not only the rich but the artisans, who pay nearly five pounds for a suit of clothes and for other luxuries in proportion. The young men rejoice in the days of their youth. They gamble, yacht, race, enjoy prize-fights and cock-fights— the one openly, the other in secret—they establish luxurious clubs; they break themselves over horse-flesh and—other things; and they are instant in quarrel. At twenty they are experienced in business; embark in vast enterprises, take partners as experienced as themselves, and go to pieces with as much splendor as their neighbors. Remember that the men who stocked California in the Fifties were physically, and as far as regards certain tough virtues, the pick of the earth. The inept and the weakly died *en route* or went under in the days of construction. To this nucleus were added all the races of the Continent—French, Italian, German, and, of course, the Jew. The result you shall see in large-boned, deep-chested, delicate-handed women, and long, elastic, well-built boys. It needs no little golden badge swinging from his watch-chain to mark the Native Son of the Golden West—the country-bred of California. Him I love because he is devoid of fear, carries himself like a man, and has a heart as big as his boots. I fancy, too, he knows how to enjoy the blessings of life that his world so abundantly bestows upon him. At least I heard a little rat of a creature with hock-bottle shoulders explaining that a man from Chicago could pull the eye-teeth of a Californian in business. Well, if I lived in

Fairyland, where cherries were as big as plums,
plums as big as apples, and strawberries of no
account; where the procession of the fruits
of the seasons was like a pageant in a Drury
Lane pantomime and where the dry air was
wine, I should let business slide once in a way
and kick up my heels with my fellows. The
tale of the resources of California—vegetable
and mineral—is a fairy tale. You can read
it in books. You would never believe me.
All manner of nourishing food from sea-fish to
beef may be bought at the lowest prices; and
the people are well developed and of a high
stomach. They demand ten shillings for tin-
kering a jammed lock of a trunk; they receive
sixteen shillings a day for working as carpen-
ters; they spend many sixpences on very bad
cigars, and they go mad over a prize-fight.
When they disagree, they do so fatally, with
fire-arms in their hands, and on the public
streets. I was just clear of Mission Street
when the trouble began between two gentlemen, one of whom perforated the other. When
a policeman, whose name I do not recollect,
"fatally shot Ed. Kearney," for attempting to
escape arrest, I was in the next street. For
these things I am thankful. It is enough to
travel with a policeman in a tram-car and while
he arranges his coat-tails as he sits down, to
catch sight of a loaded revolver. It is enough
to know that fifty per cent. of the men in the
public saloons carry pistols about them. The

Chinaman waylays his adversary and methodi-
cally chops him to pieces with his hatchet.
Then the Press roar about the brutal ferocity
of the Pagan. The Italian reconstructs his
friend with a long knife. The Press com-
plains of the waywardness of the alien. The
Irishman and the native Californian in their
hours of discontent use the revolver, not once,
but six times. The Press records the fact, and
asks in the next column whether the world can
parallel the progress of San Francisco. The
American who loves this country will tell you
that this sort of thing is confined to the lower
classes. Just at present an ex-judge who was
sent to jail by another judge (upon my word,
I cannot tell whether these titles mean anything) is breathing red-hot vengeance against
his enemy. The papers have interviewed both
parties and confidently expect a fatal issue.

Now let me draw breath and curse the negro
waiter and through him the negro in service
generally. He has been made a citizen with
a vote ; consequently both political parties
play with him. But that is neither here nor
there. He will commit in one meal every
bétise that a scullion fresh from the plow-
tail is capable of, and he will continue to repeat those faults. He is as complete a heavy-
footed, uncomprehending, bungle-fisted fool as
any *memsahib* in the East ever took into her
establishment. But he is according to law a
free and independent citizen—consequently

above reproof or criticism.   He, and he alone,
in this insane city will wait at table (the
Chinaman doesn't count).   He is untrained,
inept, but he will fill the place and draw the
pay.   Now God and his father's Kismet made
him intellectually inferior to the Oriental.   He
insists on pretending that he serves tables by
accident—as a sort of amusement.   He wishes
you to understand this little fact.   You wish
to eat your meals, and if possible to have them
properly served.   He is a big, black, vain
baby and a man rolled into one.   A colored
gentleman who insisted on getting me pie
when I wanted something else, demanded
information about India.   I gave him some
facts about wages.   "Oh hell," said he, cheer-
fully, "that wouldn't keep me in cigars for a
month."   Then he fawned on me for a ten-
cent piece.   Later he took it upon himself to
pity the natives of India—"heathen" he
called them, this Woolly One whose race has
been the butt of every comedy on the Asiatic
stage since the beginning.   And I turned and
saw by the head upon his shoulders that he
was a Yoruba man, if there be any truth in
ethnological castes.   He did his thinking in
English, but he was a Yoruba negro, and the
race type had remained the same throughout
his generations.   And the room was full of
other races—some that looked exactly like
Gallas (but the trade was never recruited
from that side of Africa), some duplicates of

Cameroon heads, and some Kroomen, if ever Kroomen wore evening dress. The American does not consider little matters of descent, though by this time he ought to know all about " damnable heredity." As a general rule he keeps himself very far from the negro and says unpretty things about him. There are six million negroes more or less in the States, and they are increasing. The Americans once having made them citizens cannot unmake them. He says, in his newspapers, they ought to be elevated by education. He is trying this: but it is like to be a long job, because black blood is much more adhesive than white, and throws back with annoying persistence. When the negro gets a religion he returns directly as a hiving bee, to the first instincts of his people. Just now a wave of religion is sweeping over some of the Southern States. Up to the present, two Messiahs and one Daniel have appeared; and several human sacrifices have been offered up to these incarnations. The Daniel managed to get three young men, who he insisted were Shadrach, Meshach, and Abednego, to walk into a blast furnace; guaranteeing non-combustion. They did not return. I have seen nothing of this kind, but I have attended a negro church. The congregation were moved by the spirit to groans and tears, and one of them danced up the aisle to the mourners' bench. The motive may have been

genuine.   The movements of the shaken body
were those of a Zanzibar stick-dance, such as
you see at Aden on the coal boats; and even
as I watched the people, the links that bound
them to the white man snapped one by one,
and I saw before me—the *hubshi* (the Woolly
One) praying to the God he did not understand.   Those neatly dressed folk on the
benches, the gray-headed elder by the window,
were savages—neither more nor less.   What
will the American do with the negro?   The
South will not consort with him.   In some
States miscegenation is a penal offense.   The
North is every year less and less in need of
his services.   And he will not disappear.   He
will continue as a problem.   His friends will
urge that he is as good as the white man.
His enemies . . . it is not good to be a negro
in the land of the free and the home of the
brave.

But this has nothing to do with San Francisco and her merry maidens, her strong,
swaggering men, and her wealth of gold and
pride.   They bore me to a banquet in honor
of a brave Lieutenant—Carlin, of the *Van-
dalia*—who stuck by his ship in the great
cyclone at Apia and comported himself as an
officer should.   On that occasion—'twas at
the Bohemian Club—I heard oratory with the
roundest of *o*'s; and devoured a dinner the
memory of which will descend with me into
the hungry grave.   There were about forty

speeches delivered ; and not one of them was average or ordinary. It was my first introduction to the American Eagle screaming for all it was worth. The Lieutenant's heroism served as a peg from which those silver-tongued ones turned themselves loose and kicked. They ransacked the clouds of sunset, the thunderbolts of Heaven, the deeps of Hell, and the splendors of the Resurrection, for tropes and metaphors, and hurled the result at the head of the guest of the evening. Never since the morning stars sang together for joy, I learned, had an amazed creation witnessed such superhuman bravery as that displayed by the American navy in the Samoa cyclone, Till earth rotted in the phosphorescent star-and-stripe slime of a decayed universe that Godlike gallantry would not be forgotten. I grieve that I cannot give the exact words. My attempt at reproducing their spirit is pale and inadequate. I sat bewildered on a coruscating Niagara of—blatherumskite. It was magnificent—it was stupendous ; and I was conscious of a wicked desire to hide my face in a napkin and grin. Then, according to rule, they produced their dead, and across the snowy tablecloths dragged the corpse of every man slain in the Civil War, and hurled defiance at " our natural enemy " (England, so please you!) " with her chain of fortresses across the world." Thereafter they glorified their nation afresh, from the beginning, in case any detail

5

should have been overlooked, and that made
me uncomfortable for their sakes.   How in
the world can a white man, a Sahib of Our
blood, stand up and plaster praise on his own
country ?   He can think as highly as he likes,
but his open-mouthed vehemence of adoration
struck me almost as indelicate.   My hosts
talked for rather more than three hours, and
at the end seemed ready for three hours more.
But when the Lieutenant—such a big, brave,
gentle giant !—rose to his feet, he delivered
what seemed to me as the speech of the evening.   I remember nearly the whole of it, and
it ran something in this way : " Gentlemen—
it's very good of you to give me this dinner
and to tell me all these pretty things, but
what I want you to understand—the fact is—
what we want and what we ought to get at
once is a navy—more ships—lots of 'em— "
Then we howled the top of the roof off, and I,
for one, fell in love with Carlin on the spot.
Wallah !   He was a man.

The Prince among merchants bade me take
no heed to the warlike sentiments of some of
the old Generals.   " The sky-rockets are
thrown in for effect," quoth he, " and whenever we get on our hind legs we always ex-
press a desire to chaw up England.   It's a
sort of family affair."

And indeed, when you come to think of it,
there is no other country for the American
public speaker to trample upon.

France has Germany ; we have Russia ; for Italy, Austria is provided ; and the humblest Pathan possesses an ancestral enemy. Only America stands out of the racket ; and therefore, to be in fashion, makes a sand-bag of the mother-country, and bangs her when occasion requires. " The chain of fortresses " man, a fascinating talker, explained to me after the affair that he was compelled to blow off steam. Everybody expected it. When we had chanted " The Star-Spangled Banner " not more than eight times, we adjourned. America is a very great country, but it is not yet Heaven with electric lights and plush fittings, as the speakers professed to believe. My listening mind went back to the politicians in the saloon who wasted no time in talking about freedom, but quietly made arrangements to impose their will on the citizens. " The Judge is a great man, but give thy presents to the Clerk," as the proverb saith.

And what more remains to tell ? I cannot write connectedly, because I am in love with all those girls aforesaid and some others who do not appear in the invoice. The type-writer girl is an institution of which the comic papers make much capital, but she is vastly convenient. She and a companion rent a room in a business quarter, and copy manuscript at the rate of six annas a page. Only a woman can manage a type-writing machine, because she has served apprenticeship to the sewing-machine. She can earn as much as a hundred dollars a month, and professes to regard this form of bread-winning as her natural destiny. But oh how she hates it in her heart of hearts! When I had got over the surprise of doing business and trying to give orders to a young woman of coldly clerkly aspect, intrenched behind gold-rimmed spectacles, I made inquiries concerning the pleasures of this independence. They liked it—indeed, they did. 'Twas the natural fate of almost all girls,—the recognized custom in America,—and I was a barbarian not to see it in that light.

" Well, and after ? " said I.   " What happens ? "

" We work for our bread."

" And then what do you expect ? "

" Then we shall work for our bread."

" Till you die ? "

" Ye-es—unless——"

" Unless what ?   A man works till he dies."

" So shall we."   This without enthusiasm —" I suppose."

Said the partner in the firm audaciously : " Sometimes we marry our employers—at least that's what the newspapers say." The hand banged on half a dozen of the keys of the machine at once. " Yes, I don't care. I hate it—I *hate* it—I hate it, and you needn't look so ! "

The senior partner was regarding the **rebel** with grave-eyed reproach.

" I thought you did," said I. " I don't suppose American girls are much different from English ones in instinct."

" Isn't it Théophile Gautier who says that the only differences between country and country lie in the slang and the uniform of the police ? "

Now in the name of all the Gods at once, what is one to say to a young lady (who in England would be a Person) who earns her own bread, and very naturally hates the employ, and slings out-of-the-way quotations at your head ? That one falls in love with her goes without saying ; but that is not enough.

A mission should be established.

V.

" I walked in the lonesome even,
     And who so sad as I,
   As I saw the young men and maidens
     Merrily passing by ? "

SAN FRANCISCO has only one drawback.
'Tis hard to leave.   When like the pious Hans
Breitmann I " cut that city by the sea " it was
with regrets for the pleasant places left behind, for the men who were so clever, and the
women who were so witty, for the " dives,"
the beer-halls, the bucket-shops, and the poker-
hells where humanity was going to the Devil
with shouting and laughter and song and the
rattle of dice-boxes.   I would fain have stayed,
but I feared that an evil end would come to
me when my money was all spent and I de-
scended to the street corner.   A voice inside
me said : " Get out of this. Go north. Strike
for Victoria and Vancouver.   Bask for a day
under the shadow of the old flag."   So I set
forth from San Francisco to Portland in
Oregon, and that was a railroad run of thirty-
six hours.

The Oakland railway terminus, whence all
the main lines start, does not own anything
approaching to a platform.   A yard with a
dozen or more tracks is roughly asphalted,

and the traveler laden with handbags skips merrily across the metals in search of his own particular train. The bells of half a dozen shunting engines are tolling suggestively in his ears. If he is run down, so much the worse for him. "When the bell rings, look out for the locomotive." Long use has made the nation familiar and even contemptuous towards trains to an extent which God never intended. Women who in England would gather up their skirts and scud timorously over a level crossing in the country, here talk dress and babies under the very nose of the cow-catcher, and little children dally with the moving car in a manner horrible to behold. We pulled out at the wholly insignificant speed of twenty-five miles an hour through the streets of a suburb of fifty thousand, and in our progress among the carts and the children and shop fronts slew nobody ; at which I was not a little disappointed.

When the negro porter bedded me up for the night and I had solved the problem of undressing while lying down,—I was much cheered by the thought that if anything happened I should have to stay where I was and wait till the kerosene lamps set the overturned car alight and burned me to death. It is easier to get out of a full theater than to leave a Pullman in haste.

By the time I had discovered that a profusion of nickel-plating, plush, and damask does not compensate for closeness and dust, the train ran into the daylight on the banks of the Sacramento River. A few windows were gingerly opened after the bunks had been reconverted into seats, but that long coffin-car was by no means ventilated, and we were a gummy, grimy crew who sat there. At six in the morning the heat was distinctly unpleasant, but seeing with the eye of the flesh that I was in Bret Harte's own country, I rejoiced. There were the pines and madrone-clad hills his miners lived and fought among; there was the heated red earth that showed whence the gold had been washed; the dry gulch, the red, dusty road where Hamblin was used to stop the stage in the intervals of his elegant leisure and superior card-play; there was the timber felled and sweating resin in the sunshine; and, above all, there was the quivering pungent heat that Bret Harte drives into your dull brain with the magic of his pen. When we stopped at a collection of packing-cases dignified by the name of a town, my felicity was complete. The name of the place was something offensive,—Amberville or Jacksonburgh,—but it owned a cast-iron fountain worthy of a town of thirty thousand. Next to the fountain was a "hotel," at least seventeen feet high including the chimney, and next to the hotel was the forest—the pine, the oak, and the untrammelled undergrowth of the hillside. A cinnamon-bear cub—Baby Sylvester in the very fur—was tied to the stump of a tree opposite the fountain ; a pack-mule dozed in the dust-haze, a red-shirted miner in a slouch hat supported the hotel, a blue-shirted miner swung round the corner, and the two went indoors for a drink. A girl came out of the only other house but one, and shading her eyes with a brown hand stared at the panting train. She didn't recognize me, but I knew her—had known her for years. She was M'liss. She never married the schoolmaster, after all, but stayed, always young and always fair, among the pines. I knew Red-Shirt too. He was one of the bearded men who stood back when Tennessee claimed his partner from the hands of the Law. The Sacramento River, a few yards away, shouted that all these things were true. The train went on while Baby Sylvester stood on his downy head, and M'liss swung her sun-bonnet by the strings.

" What do you think ? " said a lawyer who was traveling with me. " It's a new world to you; isn't it ? "

" No. It's quite familiar. I was never out of England ; it's as if I saw it all."

Quick as light came the answer : " ' Yes, they lived once thus at Venice when the miners were the kings.' "

I loved that lawyer on the spot. We drank to Bret Harte who, you remember, " claimed

California, but California never claimed him.
He's turned English."

Lying back in state, I waited for the flying
miles to turn over the pages of the book I
knew.   They brought me all I desired—from
Man of no Account sitting on a stump and
playing with a dog, to "that most sarcastic
man, the quiet Mister Brown."   He boarded
the train from out of the woods, and there
was venom and sulphur on his tongue.   He
had just lost a lawsuit.   Only Yuba Bill
failed to appear.   The train had taken his
employment from him.   A nameless ruffian
backed me into a corner and began telling me
about the resources of the country, and what
it would eventually become.   All I remember
of his lecture was that you could catch trout
in the Sacramento River—the stream that we
followed so faithfully.

Then rose a tough and wiry old man with
grizzled hair and made inquiries about the
trout.   To him was added the secretary of a
life-insurance company.   I fancy he was
traveling to rake in the dead that the train
killed.   But he, too, was a fisherman, and the
two turned to meward.   The frankness of a
Westerner is delightful.   They tell me that in
the Eastern States I shall meet another type
of man and a more reserved.   The Californian always speaks of the man from the New
England States as a different breed.   It is
our Punjab and Madras over again, but more

so. The old man was on a holiday in search of fish. When he discovered a brother-loafer he proposed a confederation of rods. Quoth the insurance-agent, "I'm not staying any time in Portland, but I will introduce you to a man there who'll tell you about fishing." The two told strange tales as we slid through the forests and saw afar off the snowy head of a great mountain. There were vineyards, fruit orchards, and wheat fields where the land opened out, and every ten miles or so, twenty or thirty wooden houses and at least three churches. A large town would have a population of two thousand and an infinite belief in its own capacities. Sometimes a flaring advertisement flanked the line, calling for men to settle down, take up the ground, and make their home there. At a big town we could pick up the local newspaper, narrow as the cutting edge of a chisel and twice as keen—a journal filled with the prices of stock, notices of improved reaping and binding machines, movements of eminent citizens —" whose fame beyond their own abode extends—for miles along the Harlem road." There was not much grace about these papers, but all breathed the same need for good men, steady men who would plow, and till, and build schools for their children, and make a township in the hills. Once only I found a sharp change in the note and a very pathetic one. I think it was a young soul in trouble who was writing poetry. The editor had jammed the verses between the flamboyant advertisement of a real-estate agent—a man who sells you land and lies about it—and that of a Jew tailor who disposed of "nobby" suits at "cut-throat prices." Here are two verses; I think they tell their own story:—

" God made the pine with its root in the earth,
   Its top in the sky;
   They have burned the pine to increase the worth
   Of the wheat and the silver rye.

" Go weigh the cost of the soul of the pine
   Cut off from the sky;
   And the price of the wheat that grows so fine
   And the worth of the silver rye!"

The thin-lipped, keen-eyed men who boarded the train would not read that poetry, or, if they did, would not understand. Heaven guard that poor pine in the desert and keep ' its top in the sky!"

When the train took to itself an extra engine and began to breathe heavily, some one said that we were ascending the Siskiyou Mountains. We had been climbing steadily from San Francisco, and at last won to over four thousand feet above sea-level, always running through forest. Then, naturally enough, we came down, but we dropped two thousand two hundred feet in about thirteen miles. It was not so much the grinding of the brakes along the train, or the sight of three curves of track apparently miles below us, or even the vision of a goods-train apparently just under our wheels, or even the tunnels, that made me reflect; it was the trestles over which we crawled,—trestles something over a hundred feet high and looking like a collection of match-sticks.

"I guess our timber is as much a curse as a blessing," said the old man from Southern California. "These trestles last very well for five or six years; then they get out of repair, and a train goes through 'em, or else a forest fire burns 'em up."

This was said in the middle of a groaning, shivering trestle. An occasional plate-layer took a look at us as we went down, but that railway didn't waste men on inspection duty. Very often there were cattle on the track, against which the engine used a diabolical form of whistling. The old man had been a driver in his youth, and beguiled the way with cheery anecdotes of what might be expected if we fouled a young calf.

"You see, they get their legs under the cow-catcher, and that'll put an engine off the line. I remember when a hog wrecked an excursion-train and killed sixty people. 'Guess the engineer will look out, though."

There is considerably too much guessing about this large nation. As one of them put it rather forcibly: "We guess a trestle will stand forever, and we guess tha. we can

patch up a washout on the track, and we
guess the road's clear, and sometimes we
guess ourselves into the deepot, and sometimes we guess ourselves into Hell."

* * * * *

The descent brought us far into Oregon
and a timber and wheat country. We drove
through wheat and pine in alternate slices, but
pine chiefly, till we reached Portland, which
is a city of fifty thousand, possessing the
electric light of course, equally, of course,
devoid of pavements, and a port of entry
about a hundred miles from the sea at which
big steamers can load. It is a poor city that
cannot say it has no equal on the Pacific
coast.   Portland shouts this to the pines
which run down from a thousand-foot ridge
clear up to the city. You may sit in a be-
dizened bar-room furnished with telephone
and clicker, and in half an hour be in the
woods.

Portland produces lumber and jig-saw fittings for houses, and beer and buggies, and
bricks and biscuit ; and, in case you should
miss the fact, there are glorified views of the
town hung up in public places with the value
of the products set down in dollars. All this
is excellent and exactly suitable to the opening
of a new country ; but when a man tells you
it is civilization, you object. The first thing
that the civilized man learns to do is to keep
the dollars in the background, because they

are only the oil of the machine that makes life go smoothly.

Portland is so busy that it can't attend to its own sewage or paving, and the four-story brick blocks front cobble-stones and plank sidewalks and other things much worse. I saw a foundation being dug out. The sewage of perhaps twenty years ago, had thoroughly soaked into the soil, and there was a familiar and Oriental look about the compost that flew up with each shovel-load. Yet the local papers, as was just and proper, swore there was no place like Portland, Oregon, U. S. A., chronicled the performances of Oregonians, "claimed" prominent citizens elsewhere as Oregonians, and fought tooth and nail for dock, rail, and wharfage projects. And you could find men who had thrown in their lives with the city, who were bound up in it, and worked their life out for what they conceived to be its material prosperity. Pity it is to record that in this strenuous, laboring town there had been, a week before, a shooting-case. One well-known man had shot another on the street, and was now pleading self-defense, because the other man had, or the murderer thought he had, a pistol about him. Not content with shooting him dead, he squibbed off his revolver into him as he lay. I read the pleadings, and they made me ill. So far as I could judge, if the dead man's body had been found with a pistol on it, the shooter would have gone free. Apart from the mere murder, cowardly enough in itself, there was a refinement of cowardice in the plea. Here in this civilized city the surviving brute was afraid he would be shot—fancied he saw the other man make a motion to his hip-pocket, and so on. Eventually the jury disagreed. And the degrading thing was that the trial was reported by men who evidently understood all about the pistol, was tried before a jury who were versed in the etiquette of the hip-pocket, and was discussed on the streets by men equally initiate.

But let us return to more cheerful things. The insurance-agent introduced us as friends to a real-estate man, who promptly bade us go up the Columbia River for a day while he made inquiries about fishing. There was no overwhelming formality. The old man was addressed as " California," I answered indifferently to " England " or " Johnny Bull," and the real-estate man was " Portland." This was a lofty and spacious form of address.

So California and I took a steamboat, and upon a sumptuous blue and gold morning steered up the Willamette River, on which Portland stands, into the great Columbia—the river that brings the salmon that goes into the tin that is emptied into the dish when the extra guest arrives in India. California introduced me to the boat and the scenery, showed me the " texas," the difference between a " tow-

head " and a " sawyer," and the precise nature
of a " slue." All I remember is a delightful
feeling that Mark Twain's Huckleberry Finn
and Mississippi Pilot were quite true, and that
I could almost recognize the very reaches
down which Huck and Jim had drifted. We
were on the border line between Oregon State
and Washington Territory, but that didn't
matter. The Columbia was the Mississippi so
far as I was concerned. We ran along the
sides of wooded islands whose banks were
caving in with perpetual smashes, and we
skipped from one side to another of the mile-
wide stream in search of a channel, exactly
like a Mississippi steamer, and when we
wanted to pick up or set down a passenger we
chose a soft and safe place on the shore and
ran our very snub nose against it. California
spoke to each new passenger as he came
aboard and told me the man's birthplace. A
long-haired tender of kine crashed out of the
underwood, waved his hat, and was taken
aboard forthwith. " South Carolina," said
California, almost without looking at him.
" When he talks you will hear a softer dialect
than mine." And it befell as he said : whereat I marveled, and California chuckled.
Every island in the river carried fields of rich
wheat, orchards, and a white, wooden-house ;
or else, if the pines grew very thickly, a saw-
mill, the tremulous whine of whose saws flickered across the water like the drone of a tired

6

bee. From remarks he let fall I gathered that
California owned timber ships and dealt in
lumber, had ranches too, a partner, and everything handsome about him ; in addition to a
checkered career of some thirty-five years.
But he looked almost as disreputable a loafer
as I.

" Say, young feller, we're going to see
scenery now. You shout and sing," said
California, when the bland wooded islands
gave place to bolder outlines, and the steamer
ran herself into a hornet's nest of black-fanged
rocks not a foot below the boiling broken
water. We were trying to get up a slue, or
back channel, by a short cut, and the stern-
wheel never spun twice in the same direction.
Then we hit a floating log with a jar that ran
through our system, and then, white-bellied,
open-gilled, spun by a dead salmon—a lordly
twenty-pound Chinook salmon who had per-
ished in his pride. " You'll see the salmon-
wheels 'fore long," said a man who lived " way
back on the Washoogle," and whose hat was
spangled with trout-flies. " Those Chinook
salmon never rise to the fly. The canneries
take them by the wheel." At the next bend
we sighted a wheel—an infernal arrangement
of wire-gauze compartments worked by the
current and moved out from a barge in shore
to scoop up the salmon as he races up the
river. California swore long and fluently at
the sight, and the more fluently when he was

told of the weight of a good night's catch—
some thousands of pounds. Think of the
black and bloody murder of it! But you out
yonder insist in buying tinned salmon, and
the canneries cannot live by letting down lines.

About this time California was struck with
madness. I found him dancing on the fore-
deck shouting, "Isn't she a daisy? Isn't she
a darling?" He had found a waterfall—a
blown thread of white vapor that broke from
the crest of a hill—a waterfall eight hundred
and fifty feet high whose voice was even
louder than the voice of the river. "Bridal
Veil," jerked out the purser. "D—n that
purser and the people who christened her!
Why didn't they call her Mechlin lace Falls at
fifty dollars a yard while they were at it?"
said California. And I agreed with him.
There are many "bridal veil" falls in this
country, but few, men say, lovelier than those
that come down to the Columbia River.
Then the scenery began—poured forth with
the reckless profusion of Nature, who when
she wants to be amiable succeeds only in being oppressively magnificent. The river was
penned between gigantic stone walls crowned
with the ruined bastions of Oriental palaces.
The stretch of green water widened and was
guarded by pine-clad hills three thousand feet
high. A wicked devil's thumb nail of rock
shot up a hundred feet in midstream. A
sand-bar of blinding white sand gave prom-

ise of flat country that the next bend denied;
for, lo! we were running under a triple tier
of fortifications, lava-topped, pine-clothed, and
terrible. Behind them the white dome of
Mount Hood ran fourteen thousand feet into
the blue, and at their feet the river threshed
among a belt of cottonwood trees. There I
sat down and looked at California half out of
the boat in his anxiety to see both sides of the
river at once. He had seen my note-book,
and it offended him. " Young feller, let her
go—and you shut your head. It's not you
nor anybody like you can put this down.
Black, the novelist, he could. He can describe salmon-fishing, *he* can." And he glared
at me as though he expected me to go and
do likewise.

"I can't. I know it," I said humbly.

" Then thank God that you came along this
way."

We reached a little railway, on an island,
which was to convey us to a second steamer,
because, as the purser explained, the river
was a "trifle broken." We had a six-mile
run, sitting in the sunshine on a dummy-
wagon, whirled just along the edge of the
river-bluffs. Sometimes we dived into the
fragrant pine woods, ablaze with flowers; but
we generally watched the river now narrowed
into a turbulent millrace. Just where the
whole body of water broke in riot over a
series of cascades, the United States Govern-

ment had chosen to build a lock for steamers, and the stream was one boiling, spouting mob of water. A log shot down the race, struck on a rock, split from end to end, and rolled over in white foam. I shuddered because my toes were not more than sixty feet above the log, and I feared that a stray splinter might have found me. But the train ran into the river on a sort of floating trestle, and I was upon another steamer ere I fully understood why. The cascades were not two hundred yards below us, and when we cast off to go upstream, the rush of the river, ere the wheel struck the water, dragged us as though we had been towed. Then the country opened out, and California mourned for his lost bluffs and crags, till we struck a rock wall four hundred feet high, crowned by the gigantic figure of a man watching us. On a rocky island we saw the white tomb of an old-time settler who had made his money in San Francisco, but who had chosen to be buried in an Indian burying-ground. A decayed wooden " wickyup," where the bones of the Indian dead are laid, almost touched the tomb. The river ran into a canal of basaltic rock, painted in yellow, vermilion, and green by Indians and, by inferior brutes, adorned with advertisements of " bile beans." We had reached The Dalles—the center of a great sheep and wool district, and the head of navigation.

When an American arrives at a new town it is his bounden duty to " take it in." California swung his coat over his shoulder with the gesture of a man used to long tramps, and together, at eight in the evening, we explored The Dalles. The sun had not yet set, and it would be light for at least another hour. All the inhabitants seemed to own a little villa and one church apiece. The young men were out walking with the young maidens, the old folks were sitting on the front steps,—not the ones that led to the religiously shuttered best drawing-room, but the side-front steps,—and the husbands and wives were tying back pear trees or gathering cherries. A scent of hay reached me, and in the stillness we could hear the cattle bells as the cows came home across the lava-sprinkled fields. California swung down the wooden pavements, audibly criticising the housewives' hollyhocks and the more perfect ways of pear-grafting, and, as the young men and maidens passed, giving quaint stories of his youth. I felt that I knew all the people aforetime, I was so interested in them and their life. A woman hung over a gate talking to another woman, and as I passed I heard her say, " skirts," and again, "skirts," and " I'll send you over the pattern "; and I knew they were talking dress. We stumbled upon a young couple saying good-by in the twilight, and " When shall I see you again ? " quoth he ; and I understood that to the doubting heart the tiny little town we paraded in twenty minutes might be as large as all London and as impassable as an armed camp. I gave them both my blessing, because " When shall I see you again?" is a question that lies very near to hearts of all the world. The last garden gate shut with a click that traveled far down the street, and the lights of the comfortable families began to shine in the confidingly uncurtained windows.

" Say, Johnny Bull, doesn't all this make you feel lonesome?" said California. "Have you got any folks at home? So've I—a wife and five children—and I'm only on a holiday."

" And I'm only on a holiday," I said, and we went back to the Spittoon-wood Hotel. Alas! for the peace and purity of the little town that I had babbled about. At the back of a shop, and discreetly curtained, was a room where the young men who had been talking to the young maidens could play poker and drink and swear, and on the shop were dime novels of bloodshed to corrupt the mind of the little boy, and prurient servant-girl-slush yarns to poison the mind of the girl. California only laughed grimly, He said that all these little one-house towns were pretty much the same all over the States.

That night I dreamed I was back in India with no place to sleep in; tramping up and down the Station mall and asking everybody, " When shall I see you again?"

VI.

"The race is neither to the swift nor the battle to the strong; but time and chance cometh to all."

I HAVE lived!

The American Continent may now sink under the sea, for I have taken the best that it yields, and the best was neither dollars, love, nor real estate.

Hear now, gentlemen of the Punjab Fishing Club, who whip the reaches of the Tavi, and you who painfully import trout to Ootacamund, and I will tell you how " old man California " and I went fishing, and you shall envy.

We returned from the Dalles to Portland by the way we had come, the steamer stopping *en route* to pick up a night's catch of one of the salmon wheels on the river, and to deliver it at a cannery down-stream.

When the proprietor of the wheel announced that his take was two thousand two hundred and thirty pounds' weight of fish, " and not a heavy catch, neither," I thought he lied. But he sent the boxes aboard, and I counted the salmon by the hundred—huge fifty-pounders, hardly dead, scores of twenty and thirty-pounders, and a host of smaller fish.

The steamer halted at a rude wooden warehouse built on piles in a lonely reach of the river, and sent in the fish. I followed them up a scale-strewn, fishy incline that led to the cannery. The crazy building was quivering with the machinery on its floors, and a glittering bank of tin-scraps twenty feet high showed where the waste was thrown after the cans had been punched. Only Chinamen were employed on the work, and they looked like blood-besmeared yellow devils, as they crossed the rifts of sunlight that lay upon the floor. When our consignment arrived, the rough wooden boxes broke of themselves as they were dumped down under a jet of water, and the salmon burst out in a stream of quicksilver. A Chinaman jerked up a twenty-pounder, beheaded and detailed it with two swift strokes of a knife, flicked out its internal arrangements with a third, and cast it into a bloody-dyed tank. The headless fish leaped from under his hands as though they were facing a rapid. Other Chinamen pulled them from the vat and thrust them under a thing like a chaff-cutter, which, descending, hewed them into unseemly red gobbets fit for the can. More Chinamen with yellow, crooked fingers, jammed the stuff into the cans, which slid down some marvelous machine forthwith, soldering their own tops as they passed. Each can was hastily tested for flaws, and then sunk, with a hundred companions, into a vat of boiling water, there to be half cooked for a few minutes. The cans bulged slightly after the operation, and were therefore slidden along by the trolleyful to men with needles and soldering irons, who vented them, and soldered the aperture. Except for the label, the "finest Columbia salmon" was ready for the market. I was impressed, not so much with the speed of the manufacture, as the character of the factory. Inside, on a floor ninety by forty, the most civilized and murderous of machinery. Outside, three footsteps, the thick-growing pines and the immense solitude of the hills. Our steamer only stayed twenty minutes at that place, but I counted two hundred and forty finished cans, made from the catch of the previous night, ere I left the slippery, blood-stained, scale-spangled, oily floors, and the offal-smeared Chinamen.

We reached Portland, California and I, crying for salmon, and the real-estate man, to whom we had been intrusted by "Portland" the insurance man, met us in the street saying that fifteen miles away, across country, we should come upon a place called Clackamas where we might perchance find what we desired. And California, his coat-tails flying in the wind, ran to a livery stable and chartered a wagon and team forthwith. I could push the wagon about with one hand, so light was its structure. The team was purely American—that is to say, almost human in its

intelligence and docility.   Some one said that
the roads were not good on the way to Clackamas and warned us against smashing the
springs.   " Portland," who had watched the
preparations, finally reckoned " he'd come
along too," and under heavenly skies we three
companions of a day set forth ; California
carefully lashing our rods into the carriage,
and the bystanders overwhelming us with
directions as to the sawmills we were to pass,
the ferries we were to cross, and the sign-posts
we were to seek signs from.   Half a mile
from this city of fifty thousand souls we struck
(and this must be taken literally) a plank-road
that would have been a disgrace to an Irish
village.

Then six miles of macadamized road showed
us that the team could move.   A railway ran
between us and the banks of the Willamette,
and another above us through the mountains.
All the land was dotted with small townships,
and the roads were full of farmers in their
town wagons, bunches of tow-haired, boggle-
eyed urchins sitting in the hay behind.   The
men generally looked like loafers, but their
women were all well dressed.   Brown hussar-
braiding on a tailor-made jacket does not,
however, consort with hay-wagons.   Then we
struck into the woods along what California
called a " *camina reale*,"—a good road,—and
Portland a " fair track."   It wound in and out
among fire-blackened stumps, under pine

trees, along the corners of log-fences, through
hollows which must be hopeless marsh in the
winter, and up absurd gradients. But nowhere throughout its length did I see any evi-
dence of road-making. There was a track,—
you couldn't well get off it,—and it was all you
could do to stay on it. The dust lay a foot
thick in the blind ruts, and under the dust we
found bits of planking and bundles of brushwood that sent the wagon bounding into the
air. Sometimes we crashed through bracken ;
anon where the blackberries grew rankest we
found a lonely little cemetery, the wooden
rails all awry, and the pitiful stumpy headstones
nodding drunkenly at the soft green mulleins.
Then with oaths and the sound of rent underwood a yoke of mighty bulls would swing down
a " skid " road, hauling a forty-foot log along
a rudely made slide. A valley full of wheat
and cherry trees succeeded, and halting at a
house we bought ten pound weight of luscious
black cherries for something less than a rupee
and got a drink of icy-cold water for nothing.
while the untended team browsed sagaciously
by the roadside. Once we found a wayside
camp of horse-dealers lounging by a pool,
ready for a sale or a swap, and once two
sun-tanned youngsters shot down a hill on
Indian ponies, their full creels banging from
the high-pommeled saddles. They had been
fishing, and were our brethren therefore. We
shouted aloud in chorus to scare a wild-cat ;

we squabbled over the reasons that had led a
snake to cross a road; we heaved bits of bark
at a venturesome chipmunk, who was really
the little gray squirrel of India and had come
to call on me; we lost our way and got the
wagon so beautifully fixed on a steep road
that we had to tie the two hind-wheels to get
it down. Above all, California told tales of
Nevada and Arizona, of lonely nights spent
out prospecting, of the slaughter of deer and
the chase of men; of woman, lovely woman,
who is a firebrand in a Western city, and
leads to the popping of pistols, and of the sudden changes and chances of Fortune, who de-
lights in making the miner or the lumberman
a quadruplicate millionaire, and in "busting"
the railroad king. That was a day to be remembered, and it had only begun when we
drew rein at a tiny farmhouse on the banks of
the Clackamas and sought horse-feed and
lodging ere we hastened to the river that
broke over a weir not a quarter of a mile
away.

Imagine a stream seventy yards broad
divided by a pebbly island, running over
seductive riffles, and swirling into deep, quiet
pools where the good salmon goes to smoke
his pipe after meals. Set such a stream amid
fields of breast-high crops surrounded by hills
of pine, throw in where you please quiet
water, log-fenced meadows, and a hundred-
foot bluff just to keep the scenery from grow-

ing too monotonous, and you will get some faint notion of the Clackamas.

Portland had no rod. He held the gaff and the whisky. California sniffed, upstream and downstream across the racing water, chose his ground, and let the gaudy spoon drop in the tail of a riffle. I was getting my rod together when I heard the joyous shriek of the reel and the yells of California, and three feet of living silver leaped into the air far across the water. The forces were engaged. The salmon tore up stream, the tense line cutting the water like a tide-rip behind him, and the light bamboo bowed to breaking. What happened after I cannot tell. California swore and prayed, and Portland shouted advice, and I did all three for what appeared to be half a day, but was in reality a little over a quarter of an hour, and sullenly our fish came home with spurts of temper, dashes head-on, and sarabands in the air; but home to the bank came he, and the remorseless reel gathered up the thread of his life inch by inch. We landed him in a little bay, and the spring-weight checked at eleven and a half pounds. Eleven and one-half pounds of fighting salmon! We danced a war-dance on the pebbles, and California caught me round the waist in a hug that went near to breaking my ribs while he shouted: "Partner!   Partner! This *is* glory! Now you catch your fish! Twenty-four years I've waited for this!"

I went into that icy-cold river and made my cast just above a weir, and all but foul-hooked a blue and black water-snake with a coral mouth who coiled herself on a stone and hissed maledictions. The next cast—ah, the pride of it, the regal splendor of it! the thrill that ran down from finger-tip to toe! The water boiled. He broke for the fly and got it! There remained enough sense in me to give him all he wanted when he jumped not once but twenty times before the upstream flight that ran my line out to the last half-dozen turns, and I saw the nickled reel-bar glitter under the thinning green coils. My thumb was burned deep when I strove to stopper the line, but I did not feel it till later, for my soul was out in the dancing water praying for him to turn ere he took my tackle away. The prayer was heard. As I bowed back, the butt of the rod on my left hip-bone and the top joint dipping like unto a weeping willow, he turned, and I accepted each inch of slack that I could by any means get in as a favor from on High. There be several sorts of success in this world that taste well in the moment of enjoyment, but I question whether the stealthy theft of line from an able-bodied salmon who knows exactly what you are doing and why you are doing it is not sweeter than any other victory within human scope. Like California's fish, he ran at me head-on and leaped against the line, but the Lord gave me two hundred and fifty pairs of fingers in that hour. The banks and the pine trees danced dizzily round me, but I only reeled— reeled as for life—reeled for hours, and at the end of the reeling continued to give him the butt while he sulked in a pool. California was farther up the reach, and with the corner of my eye I could see him casting with long casts and much skill. Then he struck, and my fish broke for the weir at the same instant, and down the reach we came, California and I; reel answering reel, even as the morning stars sung together.

The first wild enthusiasm of capture had died away. We were both at work now in deadly earnest to prevent the lines fouling, to stall off a downstream rush for deep water just above the weir, and at the same time to get the fish into the shallow bay downstream that gave the best practicable landing. Portland bade us both be of good heart, and volunteered to take the rod from my hands. I would rather have died among the pebbles than surrender my right to play and land my first salmon, weight unknown, on an eight-ounce rod. I heard California, at my ear it seemed, gasping: "He's a fighter from Fightersville, sure!" as his fish made a fresh break across the stream. I saw Portland fall off a log fence, break the overhanging bank, and clatter down to the pebbles, all sand and landing-net, and I dropped on a log to rest for

a moment. As I drew breath the weary
hands slackened their hold, and I forgot to
give him the butt. A wild scutter in the
water, a plunge and a break for the head-
waters of the Clackamas was my reward, and
the hot toil of reeling-in with one eye under
the water and the other on the top joint of
the rod, was renewed. Worst of all, I was
blocking California's path to the little landing-
bay aforesaid, and he had to halt and tire his
prize where he was. "The Father of all
Salmon!" he shouted. "For the love of
Heaven, get your *trout* to bank, Johnny Bull."
But I could no more. Even the insult failed
to move me. The rest of the game was with
the salmon. He suffered himself to be drawn,
skipping with pretended delight at getting to
the haven where I would fain have him. Yet
no sooner did he feel shoal water under his
ponderous belly than he backed like a torpedo-boat, and the snarl of the reel told me
that my labor was in vain. A dozen times at
least this happened ere the line hinted
he had given up that battle and would
be towed in. He was towed. The landing-net was useless for one of his size, and
I would not have him gaffed. I stepped
into the shallows and heaved him out with a
respectful hand under the gill, for which kindness he battered me about the legs with his
tail, and I felt the strength of him and was
proud. California had taken my place in the

shallows, his fish hard held. I was up the bank lying full length on the sweet-scented grass, and gasping in company with my first salmon caught, played and landed on an eight-ounce rod. My hands were cut and bleeding. I was dripping with sweat, spangled like harlequin with scales, wet from the waist down, nose peeled by the sun, but utterly, supremely, and consummately happy. He, the beauty, the darling, the daisy, my Salmon Bahadur, weighed twelve pounds, and I had been seven and thirty minutes bringing him to bank! He had been lightly hooked on the angle of the right jaw, and the hook had not wearied him. That hour I sat among princes and crowned heads—greater than them all. Below the bank we heard California scuffling with his salmon, and swearing Spanish oaths. Portland and I assisted at the capture, and the fish dragged the spring-balance out by the roots. It was only constructed to weigh up to fifteen pounds. We stretched the three fish on the grass,—the eleven and a half, the twelve, and fifteen pounder,—and we swore an oath that all who came after should merely be weighed and put back again.

How shall I tell the glories of that day so that you may be interested? Again and again did California and I prance down that reach to the little bay, each with a salmon in tow, and land him in the shallows. Then Portland took my rod, and caught some ten-pounders, and my spoon was carried away by an unknown leviathan. Each fish, for the merits of the three that had died so gamely, was hastily hooked on the balance and flung back, Portland recording the weight in a pocket-book, for he was a real-estate man. Each fish fought for all he was worth, and none more savagely than the smallest—a game little six-pounder. At the end of six hours we added up the list. Total: 16 fish, aggregate weight 142 lbs. The score in detail runs something like this—it is only interesting to those concerned: 15, 11½, 12, 10, 9¾, 8, and so forth; as I have said, nothing under six pounds, and three ten-pounders.

Very solemnly and thankfully we put up our rods—it was glory enough for all time—and returned weeping in each other's arms—weeping tears of pure joy—to that simple bare-legged family in the packing-case house by the waterside.

The old farmer recollected days and nights of fierce warfare with the Indians—" way back in the Fifties," when every ripple of the Columbia River and her tributaries hid covert danger. God had dowered him with a queer crooked gift of expression, and a fierce anxiety for the welfare of his two little sons—tanned and reserved children who attended school daily, and spoke good English in a strange tongue.

His wife was an austere woman who had once been kindly and perhaps handsome.

Many years of toil had taken the elasticity out of step and voice. She looked for nothing better than everlasting work—the chafing detail of housework, and then a grave somewhere up the hill among the blackberries and the pines. But in her grim way she sympathized with her eldest daughter, a small and silent maiden of eighteen, who had thoughts very far from the meals she tended or the pans she scoured.

We stumbled into the household at a crisis ; and there was a deal of downright humanity in that same. A bad, wicked dressmaker had promised the maiden a dress in time for a to-morrow's railway journey, and, though the barefooted Georgie, who stood in very wholesome awe of his sister, had scoured the woods on a pony in search, that dress never arrived. So with sorrow in her heart, and a hundred Sister Anne glances up the road, she waited upon the strangers, and, I doubt not, cursed them for the wants that stood between her and her need for tears. It was a genuine little tragedy. The mother in a heavy, passionless voice rebuked her impatience, yet sat bowed over a heap of sewing for the daughter's benefit.

These things I beheld in the long marigold-scented twilight and whispering night, loafing round the little house with California, who unfolded himself like a lotus to the moon ; or in the little boarded bunk that was our bedroom, swapping tales with Portland and the old man. Most of the yarns began in this way:

"Red Larry was a bull-puncher back of Lone County, Montana," or "There was a man riding the trail met a jack-rabbit sitting in a cactus," or "'Bout the time of the San Diego land boom, a woman from Monterey," etc.

You can try to piece out for yourselves what sort of stories they were.

And next day California took me under his wing and told me we were going to see a city smitten by a boom, and catch trout. So we took a train and killed a cow—she wouldn't get out of the way, and the locomotive "chanced" her and slew—and crossing into Washington Territory won the town of Tacoma, which stands at the head of Puget Sound upon the road to Alaska and Vancouver.

California was right. Tacoma was literally staggering under a boom of the boomiest. I do not quite remember what her natural resources were supposed to be, though every second man shrieked a selection in my ear. They included coal and iron, carrots, potatoes, lumber, shipping, and a crop of thin newspapers all telling Portland that her days were numbered. California and I struck the place at twilight. The rude boarded pavements of the main streets rumbled under the heels of hundreds of furious men all actively engaged in hunting drinks and eligible corner-lots. They sought the drinks first. The street itself alternated five-story business blocks of the later and more abominable forms of architecture with board shanties. Overhead the drunken telegraph, telephone, and electric light wires tangled on the tottering posts whose butts were half-whittled through by the knife of the loafer. Down the muddy, grimy, unmetaled thoroughfare ran a horse-car line —the metals three inches above road level. Beyond this street rose many hills, and the town was thrown like a broken set of dominoes over all. A steam tramway—it left the track the only time I used it—was nosing about the hills, but the most prominent features of the landscape were the foundations in brick and stone of a gigantic opera house and the blackened stumps of the pines. California sized up the town with one comprehensive glance. " Big boom," said he; and a few instants later: "About time to step off, *I* think," meaning thereby that the boom had risen to its limit, and it would be expedient not to meddle with it. We passed down ungraded streets that ended abruptly in a fifteen-foot drop and a nest of brambles; along pavements that beginning in pine-plank ended in the living tree; by hotels with Turkish mosque trinketry on their shameless tops, and the pine stumps at their very doors; by

a female seminary, tall, gaunt and red, which
a native of the town bade us marvel at, and
we marveled; by houses built in imitation of
the ones on Nob Hill, San Francisco,—after
the Dutch fashion; by other houses plente-
ously befouled with jig-saw work, and others
flaring with the castlemented, battlemented
bosh of the wooden Gothic school.

" You can tell just about when those fellers
had their houses built," quoth California.
" That one yonder wanted to be *I*talian, and
his architect built him what he wanted. The
new houses with the low straddle roofs and
windows pitched in sideways and red brick
walls are Dutch. That's the latest idea. I
can read the history of the town." I had no
occasion so to read. The natives were only
too glad and too proud to tell me. The hotel
walls bore a flaming panorama of Tacoma in
which by the eye of faith I saw a faint resem-
blance to the real town. The hotel stationary
advertised that Tacoma bore on its face all
the advantages of the highest civilization, and
the newspapers sang the same tune in a
louder key. The real-estate agents were selling house-lots on unmade streets miles away
for thousands of dollars. On the streets—the
rude, crude streets, where the unshaded electric light was fighting with the gentle northern
twilight—men were babbling of money, town
lots, and again money—how Alf or Ed had
done such and such a thing that had brought

him so much money; and round the corner
in a creaking boarded hall the red-jerseyed
Salvationists were calling upon mankind to
renounce all and follow their noisy God. The
men dropped in by twos and threes, listened
silently for a while, and as silently went their
way, the cymbals clashing after them in vain.
I think it was the raw, new smell of fresh
sawdust everywhere pervading the air that
threw upon me a desolating homesickness.
It brought back in a moment all remem-
brances of that terrible first night at school
when the establishment has been newly white-
washed, and a soft smell of escaping gas
mingles with the odor of trunks and wet
overcoats. I was a little boy, and the school
was very new. A vagabond among collarless
vagabonds, I loafed up the street, looking into
the fronts of little shops where they sold slop
shirts at fancy prices, which shops I saw later
described in the papers as "great." California had gone off to investigate on his own
account, and presently returned, laughing
noiselessly. "They are all mad here," he
said, "all mad. A man nearly pulled a gun
on me because I didn't agree with him that
Tacoma was going to whip San Francisco on
the strength of carrots and potatoes. I asked
him to tell me what the town produced, and I
couldn't get anything out of him except those
two darned vegetables. Say, what do you
think?"

I responded firmly, " I'm going into Brit•
ish territory a little while—to draw breath."

" I'm going up the Sound, too, for a while,"
said he, " but I'm coming back—coming back
to our salmon on the Clackamas. A man
has been pressing me to buy real estate
here. Young feller, don't you buy real
estate here."

California disappeared with a kindly wave
of his overcoat into worlds other than mine,
—good luck go with him, for he was a true
sportsman !—and I took a steamer up Puget
Sound for Vancouver, which is the terminus
of the Canadian Pacific Railway. That was a
queer voyage. The water, landlocked among
a thousand islands, lay still as oil under
our bows, and the wake of the screw broke
up the unquivering reflections of pines and
cliffs a mile away. 'Twas as though we were
trampling on glass. No one, not even the
Government, knows the number of islands in
the Sound. Even now you can get one
almost for the asking; can build a house,
raise sheep, catch salmon, and become a king
on a small scale—your subjects the Indians
of the reservation, who glide among the islets
in their canoes and scratch their hides monkey-
wise by the beach. A Sound Indian is unlovely, and only by accident picturesque.
His wife drives the canoe, but he himself is
so thorough a mariner that he can spring up
in his cockle-craft and whack his wife over

the head with a paddle without tipping the whole affair into the water. This I have seen him do unprovoked. I fancy it must have been to show off before the whites.

Have I told you anything about Seattle— the town that was burned out a few weeks ago when the insurance men at San Francisco took their losses with a grin? In the ghostly twilight, just as the forest fires were beginning to glare from the unthrifty islands, we struck it —struck it heavily, for the wharves had all been burned down, and we tied up where we could, crashing into the rotten foundations of a boat house as a pig roots in high grass. The town, like Tacoma, was built upon a hill. In the heart of the business quarters there was a horrible black smudge, as though a Hand had come down and rubbed the place smooth. I know now what being wiped out means. The smudge seemed to be about a mile long, and its blackness was relieved by tents in which men were doing business with the wreck of the stock they had saved. There were shouts and counter-shouts from the steamer to the temporary wharf, which was laden with shingles for roofing, chairs, trunks, provision-boxes, and all the lath and string arrangements out of which a western town is made. This is the way the shouts ran :—

"Oh, George! What's the best with you?"

" Nawthin'. Got the old safe out. She's
burned to a crisp. Books all gone."

"Save anythin'?"

" Bar'l o' crackers and my wife's bonnet.
Goin' to start store on them though."

" Bully for you. Where's that Emporium?
I'll drop in."

" Corner what used to be Fourth and Main
—little brown tent close to militia picquet.
Sa-ay! We're under martial law, an' all the
saloons are shut down."

"Best for you, George. Some men gets
crazy with a fire, an' liquor makes 'em crazier."

" 'Spect any creator-condemned son of a
female dog who has lost all his fixin's in a
conflagration is going to put ice on his head
an' run for Congress, do you? How'd you
like us act?"

The Job's comforter on the steamer retired
into himself.

" Oh, George" dived into the bar for a
drink.

P. S.—Among many curiosities I have unearthed one. It was a Face on a steamer—a
face above a pointed straw-colored beard, a
face with thin lips and eloquent eyes. We
conversed, and presently I got at the ideas of
the Face. It was, though it lived for nine
months of the year in the wilds of Alaska and
British Columbia, an authority on the canon
law of the Church of England—a zealous and
bitter upholder of the supremacy of the afore-

said Church. Into my amazed ears, as the steamer plodded through the reflections of the stars, it poured the battle-cry of the Church Militant here on earth, and put forward as a foul injustice that in the prisons of British Columbia the Protestant chaplain did not always belong to the Church. The Face had no official connection with the august body, and by force of his life very seldom attended service.

"But," said he, proudly, "I should think it direct disobedience to the orders of my Church if I attended any other places of worship than those prescribed. I was once for three months in a place where there was only a Wesleyan Methodist chapel, and I never set foot in it once, Sir. Never once. 'Twould have been heresy. Rank heresy."

And as I leaned over the rail methought that all the little stars in the water were shaking with austere merriment! But it may have been only the ripple of the steamer, after all.

VII.

THIS day I know how a deserter feels. Here in Victoria, a hundred and forty miles out of America, the mail brings me news from our Home—the land of regrets. I was enjoying myself by the side of a trout-stream, and I feel inclined to apologize for every rejoicing breath I drew in the diamond clear air. The sickness, they said, is heavy with you; from Rewari to the south good men are dying. Two names come in by the mail of two strong men dead—men that I dined and jested with only a little time ago, and it seems unfair that I should be here, cut off from the chain-gang and the shot-drill of our weary life. After all, there is no life like it that we lead over yonder. Americans are Americans, and there are millions of them; English are English; but we of India are Us all the world over, knowing the mysteries of each other's lives and sorrowing for the death of a brother. How can I sit down and write to you of the mere joy of being alive? The news has killed the pleasure of the day for me, and I

am ashamed of myself. There are seventy
brook trout lying in a creel, fresh drawn from
Harrison Hot Springs, and they do not con-
sole me. They are like the stolen apples that
clinch the fact of a bad boy's playing truant.
I would sell them all, with my heritage in the
woods and air and the delight of meeting new
and strange people, just to be back again in
the old galling harness, the heat and the dust,
the gatherings in the evenings by the flooded
tennis-courts, the ghastly dull dinners at the
Club when the very last woman has been
packed off to the hills and the four or five surviving men ask the doctor the symptoms of
incubating smallpox. I should be troubled in
body, but at peace in the soul. O excellent
and toil-worn public of mine—men of the
brotherhood, griffins new joined from the
February troopers, and gentlemen waiting for
your off reckonings—take care of yourselves
and keep well! It hurts so when any die.
There are so few of Us, and we know one
another too intimately.

*   *   *   *   *

Vancouver three years ago was swept off by
fire in sixteen minutes, and only one house was
left standing. To-day it has a population of
fourteen thousand people, and builds its houses
out of brick with dressed granite fronts. But
a great sleepiness lies on Vancouver as compared with an American town ; men don't fly

up and down the streets telling lies, and the spittoons in the delightfully comfortable hotel are unused ; the baths are free and their doors are unlocked. You do not have to dig up the hotel clerk when you want to bathe, which shows the inferiority of Vancouver. An American bade me notice the absence of bustle, and was alarmed when in a loud and audible voice I thanked God for it. " Give me granite —hewn granite and peace," quoth I, " and keep your deal boards and bustle for yourselves."

The Canadian Pacific terminus is not a very gorgeous place as yet, but you can be shot directly from the window of the train into the liner that will take you in fourteen days from Vancouver to Yokohama. The *Parthia*, of some five thousand tons, was at her berth when I came, and the sight of the ex-Cunard on what seemed to be a little lake was curious. Except for certain currents which are not much mentioned, but which make the entrance rather unpleasant for sailing-boats, Vancouver possesses an almost perfect harbor. The town is built all round and about the harbor, and young as it is, its streets are better than those of western America. Moreover, the old flag waves over some of the buildings, and this is cheering to the soul. The place is full of Englishmen who speak the English tongue correctly and with clearness, avoiding more blasphemy than is necessary, and taking a respectable length of time to getting outside their drinks. These advantages and others that I have heard about, such as the construction of elaborate workshops and the like by the Canadian Pacific in the near future, moved me to invest in real estate. He that sold it me was a delightful English Boy who, having tried for the Army and failed, had somehow meandered into a real-estate office, where he was doing well. I couldn't have bought it from an American. He would have overstated the case and proved me the possessor of the original Eden. All the Boy said was : " I give you my word it isn't on a cliff or under water, and before long the town ought to move out that way. I'd advise you to take it." And I took it as easily as a man buys a piece of tobacco. *Me voici*, owner of some four hundred well-developed pines, a few thousand tons of granite scattered in blocks at the roots of the pines, and a sprinkling of earth. That's a town-lot in Vancouver. You or your agent hold to it till property rises, then sell out and buy more land further out of town and repeat the process. I do not quite see how this sort of thing helps the growth of a town, but the English Boy says that it is the " essence of speculation," so it must be all right. But I wish there were fewer pines and rather less granite on my ground. Moved by curiosity and the lust of trout, I went seventy miles up the Canadian Pacific in one of the cross-Con-

tinent cars, which are cleaner and less stuffy
than the Pullman. A man who goes all the
way across Canada is liable to be disappointed
—not in the scenery, but in the progress of
the country. So a batch of wandering politicians from England told me. They even
went so far as to say that Eastern Canada was
a failure and unprofitable. The place didn't
move, they complained, and whole counties—
they said provinces—lay under the rule of the
Roman Catholic priests, who took care that
the people should not be over-cumbered with
the good things of this world to the detriment
of their souls. My interest was in the line—
the real and accomplished railway which is to
throw actual fighting troops into the East some
day when our hold of the Suez Canal is tem-
porarily loosened.

All that Vancouver wants is a fat earthwork
fort upon a hill,—there are plenty of hills to
choose from,—a selection of big guns, a couple
of regiments of infantry, and later on a big
arsenal. The raw self-consciousness of America would be sure to make her think these
arrangements intended for her benefit, but she
could be enlightened. It is not seemly to
leave unprotected the head-end of a big railway ; for though Victoria and Esquimalt, our
naval stations on Vancouver Island, are very
near, so also is a place called Vladivostok, and
though Vancouver Narrows are strait, they
allow room enough for a man-of-war. The

8

people—I did not speak to more than two hundred of them—do not know about Russia or military arrangements. They are trying to open trade with Japan in lumber, and are raising fruit, wheat, and sometimes minerals. All of them agree that we do not yet know the resources of British Columbia, and all joyfully bade me note the climate, which was distinctly warm. " We never have killing cold here. It's the most perfect climate in the world." Then there are three perfect climates, for I have tasted 'em—California, Washington Territory, and British Columbia. I cannot say which is the loveliest.

When I left by steamer and struck across the Sound to our naval station at Victoria, Vancouver Island, I found in that quite English town of beautiful streets quite a colony of old men doing nothing but talking, fishing, and loafing at the Club. That means that the retired go to Victoria. On a thousand a year pension a man would be a millionaire in these parts, and for four hundred he could live well. It was at Victoria they told me the tale of the fire in Vancouver. How the inhabitants of New Westminster, twelve miles from Vancouver, saw a glare in the sky at six in the evening but thought it was a forest fire ; how later bits of burnt paper flew about their streets, and they guessed that evil had happened ; how an hour later a man rode into the city crying that there was no Vancouver left. All had been

wiped out by the flames in sixteen minutes.
How, two hours later, the Mayor of New Westminster having voted nine thousand dollars
from the Municipal funds, relief-wagons with
food and blankets were pouring into where
Vancouver stood.   How fourteen people were
supposed to have died in the fire, but how
even now when they laid new foundations the
workmen unearthed charred skeletons, many
more than fourteen.   " That night," said the
teller, "all Vancouver was houseless.   The
wooden town had gone in a breath.   Next
day they began to build in brick, and you have
seen what they have achieved."

The sight afar off of three British men-of-
war and a torpedo-boat consoled me as I returned from Victoria to Tacoma and discovered
en route that I was surfeited with scenery.
There is a great deal in the remark of a dis-
contented traveler : " When you have seen a
fine forest, a bluff, a river, and a lake you have
seen all the scenery of western America.
Sometimes the pine is three hundred feet high,
and sometimes the rock is, and sometimes the
lake is a hundred miles long.   But it's all the
same, don't you know.   I'm getting sick of
it."   I dare not say getting sick.   I'm only
tired.   If Providence could distribute all this
beauty in little bits where people most wanted
it—among you in India,—it would be well.
But it is *en masse*, overwhelming, with nobody
but the tobacco-chewing captain of a river

steamboat to look at it.   Men said if I went
to Alaska I should see islands even more
wooded, snow-peaks loftier, and rivers more
lovely than those around me.   That decided
me not to go to Alaska.   I went east—east to
Montana, after another horrible night in Tacoma among the men who spat.   Why does
the Westerner spit?   It can't amuse him, and
it doesn't interest his neighbor.

But I am beginning to mistrust.   Everything good as well as everything bad is supposed to come from the East.   Is there a
shooting-scrape between prominent citizens?
Oh, you'll find nothing of that kind in the
East.   Is there a more than usually revolting
lynching?   They don't do that in the East.
I shall find out when I get there whether this
unnatural perfection be real.

Eastward then to Montana I took my way
for the Yellowstone National Park, called in
the guide-books "Wonderland."   But the real
Wonderland began in the train.   We were a
merry crew.   One gentleman announced his
intention of paying no fare and grappled the
conductor, who neatly cross-buttocked him
through a double plate-glass window.   His
head was cut open in four or five places.   A
doctor on the train hastily stitched up the
biggest gash, and he was dropped at a wayside station, spurting blood at every hair—a
scarlet-headed and ghastly sight.   The conductor guessed that he would die, and volun-

teered the information that there was no profit
in monkeying with the North Pacific Railway.

Night was falling as we cleared the forests
and sailed out upon a wilderness of sage brush.
The desolations of Montgomery, the wilderness
of Sind, the hummock-studded desert of Bikaneer, are joyous and homelike compared to the
impoverished misery of the sage. It is blue, it
is stunted, it is dusty. It wraps the rolling hills
as a mildewed shroud wraps the body of a
long-dead man. It makes you weep for sheer
loneliness, and there is no getting away from
it. When Childe Roland came to the dark
Tower he traversed the sage brush.

Yet there is one thing worse than sage un-
adulterated, and that is a prairie city. We
stopped at Pasco Junction, and a man told me
that it was the Queen City of the Prairie. I
wish Americans didn't tell such useless lies. I
counted fourteen or fifteen frame-houses, and
a portion of a road that showed like a bruise
on the untouched surface of the blue sage,
running away and away up to the setting sun.
The sailor sleeps with a half-inch plank between himself and death. He is at home beside the handful of people who curl themselves
up o' nights with nothing but a frail scantling,
almost as thin as a blanket, to shut out the
unmeasurable loneliness of the sage.

When the train stopped on the road, as it
did once or twice, the solid silence of the sage
got up and shouted at us. It was like a

nightmare, and one not in the least improved
by having to sleep in an emigrant-car; the
regularly ordained sleepers being full. There
was a row in our car toward morning, a man
having managed to get querulously drunk in
the night. Up rose a Cornishman with a red
head full of strategy, and strapped the obstre-
perous one, smiling. largely as he did so, and
a delicate little woman in a far bunk watched
the fray and called the drunken man a
" damned hog," which he certainly was,
though she needn't have put it quite so
coarsely. Emigrant cars are clean, but the
accommodation is as hard as a plank bed.

Later we laid our bones down to crossing
the Rockies. An American train can climb
up the side of a house if need be, but it is not
pleasant to sit in it. We clomb till we struck
violent cold and an Indian reservation, and
the noble savage came to look at us. He was
a Flathead and unlovely. Most Americans
are charmingly frank about the Indian. " Let
us get rid of him as soon as possible," they
say. " We have no use for him." Some of
the men I meet have a notion that we in India
are exterminating the native in the same
fashion, and I have been asked to fix a date
for the final extinguishment of the Aryan.
I answer that it will be a long business.
Very many Americans have an offensive habit
of referring to natives as " heathen." Ma-
hometans and Hindus are heathen alike in

their eyes, and they vary the epithet with
" pagan " and " idolater." But this is beside
the matter, which is the Stampede Tunnel—
our actual point of crossing the Rockies.
Thank Heaven, I need never take that tunnel
again ! It is about two miles long, and in
effect is nothing more than the gallery of a
mine shored with timber and lighted with
electric lamps. Black darkness would be pref-
erable, for the lamps just reveal the rough
cutting of the rocks, and that is very rough indeed. The train crawls through, brakes down,
and you can hear the water and little bits of
stone falling on the roof of the car. Then
you pray, pray fervently, and the air gets
stiller and stiller, and you dare not take your
unwilling eyes off the timber shoring, lest a
prop should fall, for lack of your moral support. Before the tunnel was built you crossed
in the open air by a switch-back line. A
watchman goes through the tunnel after each
train, but that is no protection. He just
guesses that another train will pull through,
and the engine-driver guesses the same thing.
Some day between the two of them there will
be a cave in the tunnel. Then the enterpris-
ing reporter will talk about the shrieks and
groans of the buried and the heroic efforts of
the Press in securing first information, and—
that will be all. Human life is of small account out here.

I was listening to yarns in the smoking-

compartment of the Pullman, all the way to
Helena, and with very few exceptions, each
had for its point, violent, brutal, and ruffianly
murder—murder by fraud and the craft of the
savage—murder unavenged by the law, or at
the most by an outbreak of fresh lawlessness.
At the end of each tale I was assured that the
old days had passed away, and that these
were anecdotes of five years' standing. One
man in particular distinguished himself by
holding up to admiration the exploits of some
cowboys of his acquaintance, and their skill in
the use of the revolver. Each tale of horror
wound up with " and that's the sort of man he
was," as who should say : " Go and do likewise." Remember that the shootings, the
cuttings, and the stabbings were not the outcome of any species of legitimate warfare; the
heroes were not forced to fight for their lives.
Far from it. The brawls were bred by liquor
in which they assisted—in saloons and gam-
bling-hells they were wont to " pull their guns "
on a man, and in the vast majority of cases
without provocation. The tales sickened me,
but taught one thing. A man who carries a
pistol may be put down as a coward—a person
to be shut out from every decent mess and
club, and gathering of civilized folk. There
is neither chivalry nor romance in the weapon,
for all that American authors have seen fit to
write. I would I could make you understand
the full measure of contempt with which cer

tain aspects of Western life have inspired me
Let us try a comparison. Sometimes it happens that a young, a very young, man, whose
first dress-coat is yet glossy, gets slightly
flushed at a dinner-party among his seniors.
After the ladies are gone, he begins to talk.
He talks, you will remember, as a "man of
the world" and a person of varied experiences,
an authority on all things human and divine.
The gray heads of the elders bow assentingly
to his wildest statement; some one tries to
turn the conversation when what the youngster
conceives to be wit has offended a sensibility;
and another deftly slides the decanters beyond
him as they circle round the table. You know
the feeling of discomfort—pity mingled with
aversion—over the boy who is making an
exhibition of himself. The same emotion
came back to me, when an old man who ought
to have known better appealed from time to
time for admiration of his pitiful sentiments.
It was right in his mind to insult, to maim, and
to kill; right to evade the law where it was
strong and to trample over it where it was
weak; right to swindle in politics, to lie in
affairs of State, and commit perjury in matters
of municipal administration. The car was
full of little children, utterly regardless of their
parents, fretful, peevish, spoilt beyond anything I have ever seen in Anglo-India. They
in time would grow up into men such as sat in
the smoker, and had no regard for the law,

men who would conduct papers siding " with
defiance of any and every law." But it's of
no consequence, as Mr. Toots says.

During the descent of the Rockies we journeyed for a season on a trestle only two hundred and eighty-six feet high. It was made of
iron, but up till two years ago a wooden structure bore up the train, and was used long after
it had been condemned by the civil engineers.
Some day the iron one will come down, just
as Stampede Tunnel will, and the results will
be even more startling.

Late in the night we ran over a skunk—
ran over it in the dark. Everything that has
been said about the skunk is true. It is an
Awesome Stink.

VIII.

LIVINGSTONE is a town of two thousand
people, and the junction for the little side-line
that takes you to the Yellowstone National
Park.   It lies in a fold of the prairie, and behind it is the Yellowstone River and the gate
of the mountains through which the river
flows.   There is one street in the town, where
the cowboy's pony and the little foal of the
brood-mare in the buggy rest contentedly in
the blinding sunshine while the cowboy gets
himself shaved at the only other barber's shop,
and swaps lies at the bar.   I exhausted the
town, including the saloons, in ten minutes,
and got away on the rolling grass downs where
I threw myself to rest.   Directly under the
hill I was on, swept a drove of horses in charge
of two mounted men.   That was a picture I
shall not soon forget.   A light haze of dust
went up from the hoof-trodden green, scarcely
veiling the unfettered deviltries of three hundred horses who very much wanted to stop
and graze.   "Yow! Yow! Yow!" yapped
the mounted men in chorus like coyotes.   The
column moved forward at a trot, divided as it
met a hillock and scattered into fan shape all
among the suburbs of Livingstone.   I heard
the "snick" of a stock whip, half a dozen

" Yow, yows," and the mob had come together again, and, with neighing and wickering and squealing and a great deal of kicking on the part of the youngsters, rolled like a wave of brown water toward the uplands.

I was within twenty feet of the leader, a gray stallion — lord of many brood-mares all deeply concerned for the welfare of their fuzzy foals. A cream-colored beast—I knew him at once for the bad character of the troop—broke back, taking with him some frivolous fillies. I heard the snick of the whips somewhere in the dust, and the fillies came back at a canter, very shocked and in-dignant. On the heels of the last rode both the stockmen — picturesque ruffians who wanted to know "what in hell" I was doing there, waved their hats, ard swept down the slope after their charges. When the noise of the troop had died there came a wonderful silence on all the prairie—that silence, they say, which enters into the heart of the old-time hunter and trapper and marks him off from the rest of his race. The town disap-peared in the darkness, and a very young moon showed herself over a bald-headed, snow-flecked peak. Then the Yellowstone, hidden by the water-willows, lifted up its voice and sang a little song to the mountains, and an old horse that had crept up in the dusk breathed inquiringly on the back of my neck. When I reached the hotel I found all manner of preparation under way for the 4th of July, and a drunken man with a Winchester rifle over his shoulder patrolling the sidewalk. I do not think he wanted any one. He carried the gun as other folk carry walking-sticks. None the less I avoided the direct line of fire and listened to the blasphemies of miners and stockmen till far into the night. In every bar-room lay a copy of the local paper, and every copy impressed it upon the inhabitants of Livingstone that they were the best, finest, bravest, richest, and most progressive town of the most progressive nation under Heaven ; even as the Tacoma and Portland papers had belauded their readers. And yet, all my purblind eyes could see was a grubby little hamlet full of men without clean collars and perfectly unable to get through one sentence unadorned by three oaths. They raise horses and minerals round and about Livingstone, but they behave as though they raised cherubims with diamonds in their wings.

From Livingstone the National Park train follows the Yellowstone River through the gate of the mountains and over arid volcanic country. A stranger in the cars saw me look at the ideal trout-stream below the windows and murmured softly : " Lie off at Yankee Jim's if you want good fishing." They halted the train at the head of a narrow valley, and I leaped literally into the arms of Yankee Jim, sole owner of a log hut and an indefinite amount of hay-ground, and constructor of twenty-seven miles of wagon-road over which he held toll right. There was the hut—the river fifty yards away, and the polished line of metals that disappeared round a bluff. That was all. The railway added the finishing touch to the already complete loneliness of the place. Yankee Jim was a picturesque old man with a talent for yarns that Annanias might have envied. It seemed to me, presumptuous in my ignorance, that I might hold my own with the old-timer if I judiciously painted up a few lies gathered in the course of my wanderings. Yankee Jim saw every one of my tales and went fifty better on the spot. He dealt in bears and Indians— never less than twenty of each; had known the Yellowstone country for years, and bore upon his body marks of Indian arrows; and his eyes had seen a squaw of the Crow Indians burned alive at the stake. He said she screamed considerable. In one point did he speak the truth—as regarded the merits of that particular reach of the Yellowstone. He said it was alive with trout. It was. I fished it from noon till twilight, and the fish bit at the brown hook as though never a fat trout-fly had fallen on the water. From pebbly reaches, quivering in the heat-haze where the foot caught on stumps cut four-square by the chisel-tooth of the beaver; past the fringe of the water-willow crowded with the breeding trout-fly and alive with toads and water-snakes ; over the drifted timber to the grate-ful shadow of big trees that darkened the holes where the fattest fish lay, I worked for seven hours. The mountain flanks on either side of the valley gave back the heat as the desert gives it, and the dry sand by the rail-way track, where I found a rattlesnake, was hot-iron to the touch. But the trout did not care for the heat. They breasted the boiling river for my fly and they got it. I simply dare not give my bag. At the fortieth trout I gave up counting, and I had reached the fortieth in less than two hours. They were small fish,—not one over two pounds,—but they fought like small tigers, and I lost three flies before I could understand their methods of escape. Ye gods! That was fishing, though it peeled the skin from my nose in strips.

At twilight Yankee Jim bore me off, pro-testing, to supper in the hut. The fish had prepared me for any surprise, wherefore when Yankee Jim introduced me to a young woman of five-and-twenty, with eyes like the deep-fringed eyes of the gazelle, and " on the neck the small head buoyant, like a bell-flower in its bed," I said nothing. It was all in the day's events. She was California-raised, the wife of a man who owned a stock-farm " up the river a little ways," and, with her husband, tenant of Yankee Jim's shanty. I know she wore list slippers, and did not wear stays ; but I know also that she was beautiful by any standard of beauty, and that the trout she cooked were fit for a king's supper. And after supper strange men loafed up in the dim delicious twilight, with the little news of the day—how a heifer had " gone strayed " from Nicholson's ; how the widow at Grant's Fork wouldn't part with a little hayland nohow, though " she an' her big brothers can't manage more than ha-af of their land now. She's so darned proud." Diana of the Crossways entertained them in queenly wise, and her husband and Yankee Jim bade them sit right down and make themselves at home. Then did Yankee Jim uncurl his choicest lies on Indian warfare aforetime ; then did the whisky-flask circle round the little crowd ; then did Diana's husband 'low that he was quite handy with the lariat, but had seen men rope a steer by any foot or horn indicated ; then did Diana unburden herself about her neighbors. The nearest house was three miles away, " but the women aren't nice, neighborly folk. They talk so. They haven't got anything else to do, seemingly. If a woman goes to a dance and has a good time, they talk, and if she wears a silk dress, they want to know how jest ranchin' folks—folk on a ranche—come by such things ; and they make mischief down all the lands here from Gardiner City way back up to Livingstone. They're mostly

Montana raised, and they haven't been no-
wheres. Ah, how they talk ! " " Were things
like this," demanded Diana, " in the big world
outside, whence I had come ? " " Yes," I
said, "' things were very much the same all
over the world," and I thought of a far-away
station in India, where new dresses and the
having of good times at dances raised cackle
more grammatical perhaps, but no less veno-
mous than the gossip of the " Montana-raised "
folk on the ranches of the Yellowstone.

Next morn I fished again and listened to
Diana telling the story of her life. I forget
what she told me, but I am distinctly aware
that she had royal eyes and a mouth that the
daughter of a hundred earls might have envied
—so small and so delicately cut it was. " An'
you come back an' see us again," said the
simple-minded folk. " Come back an' we'll
show you how to catch six-pound trout at the
head of the cañon."

To-day I am in the Yellowstone Park, and I
wish I were dead. The train halted at Cin-
nabar station, and we were decanted, a howling crowd of us, into stages, variously horsed,
for the eight-mile drive to the first spectacle of
the Park—a place called the Mammoth Hot
Springs. " What means this eager, anxious
throng ? " I asked the driver. " You've struck
one of Rayment's excursion parties—that's
all—a crowd of creator-condemned fools
mostly. Aren't you one of 'em ? " " No," I

said.   "May I sit up here with you, great chief and man with a golden tongue?   I do not know Mister Rayment.   I belong to T. Cook and Son."   The other person, from the quality of the material he handles, must be the son of a sea-cook.   He collects masses of Down-Easters from the New England States and elsewhere and hurls them across the Continent and into the Yellowstone Park on tour.   A brake-load of Cook's Continental tourists tra-pezing through Paris (I've seen 'em) are angels of light compared to the Rayment trippers. It is not the ghastly vulgarity, the oozing, rampant Bessemer-steel self-sufficiency and ignorance of the men that revolts me, so much as the display of these same qualities in the women-folk.   I saw a new type in the coach, and all my dreams of a better and more per-fect East died away.   "Are these—um—per-sons here any sort of persons in their own places?"   I asked a shepherd who appeared to be herding them.

"Why, certainly.   They include very many prominent and representative citizens from seven States of the Union, and most of them are wealthy.   Yes, *sir*.   Representative and prominent."

We ran across bare hills on an unmetaled road under a burning sun in front of a volley of playful repartee from the prominent citizens inside.   It was the 4th of July.   The horses had American flags in their headstalls, some

of the women wore flags and colored hand-
kerchiefs in their belts, and a young German
on the box-seat with me was bewailing the loss
of a box of crackers. He said he had been
sent to the Continent to get his schooling and so
had lost his American accent; but no Continental schooling writes German Jew all over a
man's face and nose. He was a rabid American
citizen—one of a very difficult class to deal
with. As a general rule, praise unsparingly,
and without discrimination. That keeps most
men quiet ; but some, if you fail to keep up a
continuous stream of praise, proceed to revile
the Old Country—Germans and Irish who
are more Americans than the Americans are
the chief offenders. This young American
began to attack the English army. He had
seen some of it on parade and he pitied the
men in bearskins as " slaves." The citizen,
by the way, has a contempt for his own army
which exceeds anything you meet among the
most illiberal classes in England. I admitted
that our army was very poor, had done nothing, and had been nowhere. This exasper-
ated him, for he expected an argument, and
he trampled on the British Lion generally.
Failing to move me, he vowed that I had no
patriotism like his own. I said I had not, and
further ventured that very few Englishmen
had ; which, when you come to think of it, is
quite true. By the time he had proved conclusively that before the Prince of Wales came

to the throne we should be a blethering republic, we struck a road that overhung a river,
and my interest in " politics " was lost in admiration of the driver's skill as he sent his
four big horses along that winding road.
There was no room for any sort of accident—
a shy or a swerve would have dropped us
sixty feet into the roaring Gardiner River.
Some of the persons in the coach remarked
that the scenery was " elegant." Wherefore,
even at the risk of my own life, I did urgently
desire an accident and the massacre of some
of the more prominent citizens. What " ele-
gance " lies in a thousand-foot pile of honey-
colored rock, riven into peak and battlement,
the highest peak defiantly crowned by an
eagle's nest, the eaglet peering into the gulf
and screaming for his food, I could not for
the life of me understand. But they speak a
strange tongue.

En route we passed other carriages full of
trippers, who had done their appointed five
days in the Park, and yelped at us fraternally
as they disappeared in clouds of red dust.
When we struck the Mammoth Hot Spring
Hotel—a huge yellow barn—a sign-board informed us that the altitude was six thousand
two hundred feet. The Park is just a howling
wilderness of three thousand square miles,
full of all imaginable freaks of a fiery nature.
An hotel company, assisted by the Secretary
of State for the Interior, appears to control it;

there are hotels at all the points of interest, guide-books, stalls for the sale of minerals, and so forth, after the model of Swiss summer places.

The tourists—may their master die an evil death at the hand of a mad locomotive!—poured into that place with a joyful whoop, and, scarce washing the dust from themselves, began to celebrate the 4th of July. They called it "patriotic exercises"; elected a clergyman of their own faith as president, and, sitting on the landing of the first floor, began to make speeches and read the Declaration of Independence. The clergyman rose up and told them they were the greatest, freest, sub-limest, most chivalrous, and richest people on the face of the earth, and they all said Amen. Another clergyman asserted in the words of the Declaration that all men were created equal, and equally entitled to Life, Liberty, and the pursuit of Happiness. I should like to know whether the wild and woolly West recognizes this first right as freely as the grantors intended. The clergyman then bade the world note that the tourists included rep-resentatives of seven of the New England States; whereat I felt deeply sorry for the New England States in their latter days. He opined that this running to and fro upon the earth, under the auspices of the excellent Rayment, would draw America more closely together, especially when the Westerners remembered the perils that they of the East had surmounted by rail and river. At duly appointed intervals the congregation sang " My country, 'tis of thee " to the tune of " God save the Queen " (here they did not stand up), and the " Star-Spangled Banner " (here they did), winding up the exercise with some doggrel of their own composition to the tune of " John Brown's body," movingly setting forth the perils before alluded to. They then adjourned to the verandas and watched firecrackers of the feeblest, exploding one by one, for several hours.

What amazed me was the calm with which these folks gathered together and commenced to belaud their noble selves, their country, and their " institootions " and everything else that was theirs. The language was, to these bewildered ears, wild advertisement, gas, bunkum, blow, anything you please beyond the bounds of common sense. An archangel, selling town-lots on the Glassy Sea, would have blushed to the tips of his wings to describe his property in similar terms. Then they gathered round the pastor and told him his little sermon was " perfectly glorious," really grand, sublime, and so forth, and he bridled ecclesiastically. At the end a perfectly unknown man attacked me and asked me what I thought of American patriotism. I said there was nothing like it in the Old Country. By the way, always tell an American this. It soothes him.

Then said he: " Are you going to get out your letters—your letters of naturalization ? "

" Why ? " I asked.

" I presoom you do business in this country, and make money out of it,—and it seems to me that it would be your dooty."

" Sir," said I, sweetly, " there is a forgotten little isle across the seas called England. It is not much bigger than the Yellowstone Park. In that island a man of your country could work, marry, make his fortune or twenty fortunes, and die. Throughout his career not one soul would ask him whether he were a British subject or a child of the Devil. Do you understand ? "

I think he did, because he said something about " Britishers " which wasn't complimentary.

IX.

"That desolate land and lone
    Where the Big Horn and Yellowstone
    Roar down their mountain path."

TWICE have I written this letter from end
to end. Twice have I torn it up, fearing lest
those across the water should say that I had
gone mad on a sudden. Now we will begin
for the third time quite solemnly and soberly.
I have been through the Yellowstone National
Park in a buggy, in the company of an adventurous old lady from Chicago and her
husband, who disapproved of scenery as being
" ongodly." I fancy it scared them.

We began, as you know, with the Mammoth Hot Springs. They are only a gigantic
edition of those pink and white terraces not
long ago destroyed by earthquake in New
Zealand. At one end of the little valley in
which the hotel stands the lime-laden springs
that break from the pine-covered hillsides
have formed a frozen cataract of white, lemon,
and palest pink formation, through and over
and in which water of the warmest bubbles
and drips and trickles from pale-green lagoon
to exquisitely fretted basin. The ground
rings hollow as a kerosene-tin, and some day
the Mammoth Hotel, guests and all, will sink

into the caverns below and be turned into a stalactite. When I set foot on the first of the terraces, a tourist-trampled ramp of scabby gray stuff, I met a stream of iron-red hot water which ducked into a hole like a rabbit. Followed a gentle chuckle of laughter, and then a deep, exhausted sigh from nowhere in particular. Fifty feet above my head a jet of stream rose up and died out in the blue. It was worse than the boiling mountain at Myanoshita. The dirty white deposit gave place to lime whiter than snow; and I found a basin which some learned hotel-keeper has christened Cleopatra's pitcher, or Mark Antony's whisky-jug, or something equally poetical. It was made of frosted silver; it was filled with water as clear as the sky. I do not know the depth of that wonder. The eye looked down beyond grottoes and caves of beryl into an abyss that communicated directly with the central fires of earth. And the pool was in pain, so that it could not refrain from talking about it; muttering and chattering and moaning. From the lips of the lime-ledges, forty feet under water, spurts of silver bubbles would fly up and break the peace of the crystal atop. Then the whole pool would shake and grow dim, and there were noises. I removed myself only to find other pools all equally unhappy, rifts in the ground, full of running, red-hot water, slippery sheets of deposit overlaid with greenish gray hot water, and here and there pit-holes dry as a rifled tomb in India, dusty and waterless. Elsewhere the infernal waters had first boiled dead and then embalmed the pines and underwood, or the forest trees had taken heart and smothered up a blind formation with greenery, so that it was only by scraping the earth you could tell what fires had raged beneath. Yet the pines will win the battle in years to come, because Nature, who first forges all her work in her great smithies, has nearly finished this job, and is ready to temper it in the soft brown earth. The fires are dying down; the hotel is built where terraces have overflowed into flat wastes of deposits; the pines have taken possession of the high ground whence the terraces first started. Only the actual curve of the cataract stands clear, and it is guarded by soldiers who patrol it with loaded six-shooters, in order that the tourist may not bring up fence-rails and sink them in a pool, or chip the fretted tracery of the formations with a geological hammer, or, walking where the crust is too thin, foolishly cook himself.

I maneuvered round those soldiers. They were cavalry in a very slovenly uniform, dark-blue blouse, and light-blue trousers unstrapped, cut spoon-shape over the boot; cartridge belt, revolver, peaked cap, and worsted gloves —black buttons ! By the mercy of Allah I opened conversation with a spectacled Scot.

He had served the Queen in the Marines and
a Line regiment, and the " go-fever " being in
his bones, had drifted to America, there to
serve Uncle Sam. We sat on the edge of an
extinct little pool, that under happier circumstances would have grown into a geyser, and
began to discuss things generally. To us
appeared yet another soldier. No need to ask
his nationality or to be told that the troop
called him " The Henglishman." A cockney
was he, who had seen something of warfare in
Egypt, and had taken his discharge from a
Fusilier regiment not unknown to you.

" And how do things go ? "

" Very much as you please," said they.
" There's not half the discipline here that
there is in the Queen's service—not half—nor
the work either, but what there is, is rough
work. Why, there's a sergeant now with a
black eye that one of our men gave him.
They won't say anything about that, of course.
Our punishments ? Fines mostly, and then if
you carry on too much you go to the cooler—
that's the clink. Yes, Sir. Horses ? Oh,
they're devils, these Montana horses. Bron-
chos mostly. We don't slick 'em up for
parade—not much. And the amount of
schooling that you put into one English troop-
horse would be enough for a whole squadron
of these creatures. You'll meet more troopers
further up the Park. Go and look at their
horses and their turnouts. I fancy it'll startle

you. I'm wearing a made tie and a breastpin under my blouse ? Of course I am ! I can wear anything I darn please. We aren't particular here. I shouldn't dare come on parade —no, nor yet fatigue duty—in this condition in the Old Country ; but it don't matter here. But don't you forget, Sir, that it's taught me how to trust to myself, and my shooting irons. I don't want fifty orders to move me across the Park, and catch a poacher. Yes, they poach here. Men come in with an outfit and ponies, smuggle in a gun or two, and shoot the bison. If you interfere, they shoot at you. Then you confiscate all their outfit and their ponies. We have a pound full of them now down below. There's our Captain over yonder. Speak to him if you want to know anything special. This service isn't a patch on the Old Country's service ; but you look, if it was worked up it would be just a Hell of a service. But these citizens despise us, and they put us on to road-mending, and such like. 'Nough to ruin any army."

To the Captain I addressed myself after my friends had gone. They told me that a good many American officers dressed by the French army. The Captain certainly might have been mistaken for a French officer of light cavalry, and he had more than the courtesy of a Frenchman. Yes, he had read a good deal about our Indian border warfare, and had been much struck with the likeness it bore to

Red Indian warfare. I had better, when I reached the next cavalry post, scattered between two big geyser basins, introduce myself to a Captain and Lieutenant. They could show me things. He himself was devoting all his time to conserving the terraces, and surreptitiously running hot water into dried-up basins that fresh pools might form. " I get very interested in that sort of thing. It's not duty, but it's what I'm put here for." And then he began to talk of his troop as I have heard his brethren in India talk. Such a troop ! Built up carefully, and watched lovingly : " not a man that I'd wish to exchange, and, what's more, I believe not a man that would wish to leave on his own account. We're different, I believe, from the English. Your officers value the horses ; we set store on the men. We train them more than we do the horses."

Of the American trooper I will tell you more hereafter. He is not a gentleman to be trifled with.

Next dawning, entering a buggy of fragile construction, with the old people from Chicago, I embarked on my perilous career. We ran straight up a mountain till we could see, sixty miles away, the white houses of Cook City on another mountain, and the whiplash-like trail leading thereto. The live air made me drunk. If Tom, the driver, had proposed to send the mares in a bee-line to the city, I should have assented, and so would the old lady, who

chewed gum and talked about her symptoms.
The tub-ended rock-dog, which is but the
translated prairie-dog, broke across the road
under our horses' feet, the rabbit and the chipmunk danced with fright ; we heard the roar
of the river, and the road went round a corner.
On one side piled rock and shale, that en-
joined silence for fear of a general slide-down ;
on the other a sheer drop, and a fool of a noisy
river below. Then, apparently in the middle
of the road, lest any should find driving too
easy, a post of rock. Nothing beyond that
save the flank of a cliff. Then my stomach
departed from me, as it does when you swing,
for we left the dirt, which was at least some
guarantee of safety, and sailed out round the
curve, and up a steep incline, on a plank-road
built out from the cliff. The planks were
nailed at the outer edge, and did not shift or
creak very much—but enough, quite enough.
That was the Golden Gate. I got my stomach
back again when we trotted out on to a vast
upland adorned with a lake and hills. Have
you ever seen an untouched land—the face of
virgin Nature ? It is rather a curious sight,
because the hills are choked with timber that
has never known an ax, and the storm has
rent a way through this timber, so that a hundred thousand trees lie matted together in
swathes ; and, since each tree lies where it
falls, you may behold trunk and branch returning to the earth whence they sprang—exactly

as the body of man returns—each limb making
its own little grave, the grass climbing above
the bark, till at last there remains only the
outline of a tree upon the rank undergrowth.

Then we drove under a cliff of obsidian,
which is black glass, some two hundred feet
high; and the road at its foot was made of
black glass that crackled. This was no great
matter, because half an hour before Tom had
pulled up in the woods that we might suffi-
ciently admire a mountain who stood all by
himself, shaking with laughter or rage.

The glass cliff overlooks a lake where the
beavers built a dam about a mile and a half
long in a zig-zag line, as their necessities
prompted. Then came the Government and
strictly preserved them, and, as you shall learn
later on, they be damn impudent beasts. The
old lady had hardly explained the natural history of beavers before we climbed some hills—
it really didn't matter in that climate, because
we could have scaled the stars—and (this
mattered very much indeed) shot down a
desperate, dusty slope, brakes shrieking on
the wheels, the mares clicking among unseen
rocks, the dust dense as a fog, and a wall of
trees on either side. "How do the heavy
four-horse coaches take it, Tom?" I asked,
remembering that some twenty-three souls had
gone that way half an hour before. "Take it
at the run!" said Tom, spitting out the dust.
Of course there was a sharp curve, and a bridge

at the bottom, but luckily nothing met us, and we came to a wooden shanty called an hotel, in time for a crazy tiffin served by very gorgeous handmaids with very pink cheeks. When health fails in other and more exciting pursuits, a season as " help " in one of the Yellowstone hotels will restore the frailest constitution.

Then by companies after tiffin we walked chattering to the uplands of Hell.   They call it the Norris Geyser Basin on Earth.   It was as though the tide of desolation had gone out, but would presently return, across innumerable acres of dazzling white geyser formation. There were no terraces here, but all other horrors.   Not ten yards from the road a blast of steam shot up roaring every few seconds, a mud volcano spat filth to Heaven, streams of hot water rumbled under foot, plunged through the dead pines in steaming cataracts and died on a waste of white where green-gray, black-yellow, and link pools roared, shouted, bubbled, or hissed as their wicked fancies prompted. By the look of the eye the place should have been frozen over.   By the feel of the feet it was warm.   I ventured out among the pools, carefully following tracks, but one unwary foot began to sink, a squirt of water followed, and having no desire to descend quick into Tophet I returned to the shore where the mud and the sulphur and the nameless fat ooze-vegetation of Lethe lay.   But the very road rang as though built over a gulf ; and besides, how was I to tell when the raving blast of steam would find its vent insufficient and blow the whole affair into Nirvana ?   There was a po- tent stench of stale eggs everywhere, and crystals of sulphur crumbled under the foot, and the glare of the sun on the white stuff was blinding.   Sitting under a bank, to me appeared a young trooper—ex-Cape mounted Rifles, this man : the real American seems to object to his army—mounted on a horse half- maddened by the noise and steam and smell. He carried only the six-shooter and cartridge- belt.   On service the Springfield carbine (which is clumsy) and a cartridge-belt slung diagonally complete equipment.   The sword is no earthly use for Border warfare and, ex- cept at state parades, is never worn.   The saddle is the McClellan tree over a four- folded blanket.   Sweat-leathers you must pay for yourself.   And the beauty of the tree is that it necessitates first very careful girthing and a thorough knowledge of tricks with the blanket to suit the varying conditions of the horse—a broncho will bloat in a night if he can get at a bellyful—and, secondly, even more careful riding to prevent galling.   Crup- per and breast-band do not seem to be used,— but they are casual about their accouterments, —and the bit is the single, jaw-breaking curb which American war-pictures show us.   That young man was very handsome, and the gray

10

service hat—most like the under half of a
seedy terai—shaded his strong face admirably
as his horse backed and shivered and sidled
and plunged all over the road, and he lectured
from his saddle, one foot out of the heavy-
hooded stirrup, one hand on the sweating
neck. " He's not used to the Park, this brute,
and he's a confirmed bolter on parade ; but
we understand each other." *Whoosh!* went
the steam-blast down the road with a dry roar.
Round spun the troop horse prepared to bolt,
and, his momentum being suddenly checked,
reared till I thought he would fall back on his
rider. " Oh, no ; we settled that little matter when I was breaking him," said Centaur.
" He used to try to fall back on me. Isn't he
a devil ? I think you'd laugh to see the way
our regiments are horsed. Sometimes a big
Montana beast like mine has a thirteen-two
broncho pony for neighbor, and it's annoying
if you're used to better things. And oh, how
you have to ride your mount ! It's necessary ;
but I can tell you at the end of a long day's
march, when you'd give all the world to ride
like a sack, it isn't sweet to get extra drill for
slouching. When we're turned out, we're
turned out for *anything*—not a fifteen-mile
trot, but for the use and behoof of all the
Northern States. I've been in Arizona. A
trooper there who had been in India told me
that Arizona was like Afghanistan. There's
nothing under Heaven there except horned

toads and rattlesnakes—and Indians. Our
trouble is that we only deal with Indians and
they don't teach us much, and of course the
citizens look down on us and all that. As a
matter of fact, I suppose we're really only
mounted infantry, but remember we're the
best mounted infantry in the world." And
the horse danced a fandango in proof.

"My faith!" said I, looking at the dusty
blouse, gray hat, soiled leather accouterments,
and whalebone poise of the wearer. "If they
are all like you, you are."

"Thanks, whoever you may be. Of course
if we were turned into a lawn-tennis court and
told to resist, say, your heavy cavalry, we'd
be ridden off the face of the earth if we
couldn't get away. We have neither the
weight nor the drill for a charge. My horse,
for instance, by English standards, is half-
broken, and like all the others, he bolts when
we're in line. But cavalry charge against
cavalry charge doesn't happen often, and if it
did, well—all our men know that up to a hundred yards they are absolutely safe behind
this old thing." He patted his revolver pouch.
"Absolutely safe from any shooting of yours.
What man do you think would dare to use a
pistol at even thirty yards, if his life depended
on it? Not one of *your* men. They can't
shoot. We can. You'll hear about that down
the Park—further up."

Then he added, courteously: "Just now it

seems that the English supply all the men to
the American Army. That's what makes
them so good perhaps." And with mutual
expressions of good-will we parted—he to an
outlying patrol fifteen miles away, I to my
buggy and the old lady, who, regarding the
horrors of the fire-holes, could only say,
"Good Lord!" at thirty-second intervals.
Her husband talked about "dreffel waste of
steam-power," and we went on in the clear,
crisp afternoon, speculating as to the formation of geysers.

"What I say," shrieked the old lady *apropos*
of matters theological, "and what I say more,
after having seen all that, is that the Lord has
ordained a Hell for such as disbelieve His
gracious works."

Nota bene.—Tom had profanely cursed the
near mare for stumbling. He looked straight
in front of him and said no word, but the left
corner of his left eye flickered in my direction.

"And if," continued the old lady, "if we
find a thing so dreffel as all that steam and
sulphur allowed on the face of the earth,
mustn't we believe that there is something ten
thousand times more terrible below prepared
un*toe* our destruction?"

Some people have a wonderful knack of
extracting comfort from things. I am
ashamed to say I agreed ostentatiously with
the old lady. She developed the personal
view of the matter.

"*Now* I shall be able to say something to Anna Fincher about her way of living. Shan't I, Blake?" This to her husband.

"Yes," said he, speaking slowly after a heavy tiffin. "But the girl's a good girl;" and they fell to arguing as to whether the luckless Anna Fincher really stood in need of lectures edged with Hell fire (she went to dances, I believe), while I got out and walked in the dust alongside of Tom.

"I drive blame cur'ous kinder folk through this place," said he. "Blame cur'ous. 'Seems a pity that they should ha' come so far just to liken Norris Basin to Hell. 'Guess Chicago would ha' served 'em, speaking in comparison, jest as good."

We curved the hill and entered a forest of spruce, the path serpentining between the tree-boles, the wheels running silent on immemorial mold. There was nothing alive in the forest save ourselves. Only a river was speaking angrily somewhere to the right. For miles we drove till Tom bade us alight and look at certain falls. Wherefore we stepped out of that forest and nearly fell down a cliff which guarded a tumbled river and returned demanding fresh miracles. If the water had run up-hill, we should perhaps have taken more notice of it; but 'twas only a waterfall, and I really forget whether the water was warm or cold. There is a stream here called Firehole River. It is fed by the overflow

from the various geysers and basins,—a warm
and deadly river wherein no fish breed. I
think we crossed it a few dozen times in the
course of a day.

Then the sun began to sink, and there was
a taste of frost about, and we went swiftly
from the forest into the open, dashed across
a branch of the Firehole River and found a
wood shanty, even rougher than the last at
which, after a forty-mile drive, we were to dine
and sleep. Half a mile from this place stood,
on the banks of the Firehole River, a " beaver-
lodge," and there were rumors of bears and
other cheerful monsters in the woods on the
hill at the back of the building.

In the cool, crisp quiet of the evening I
sought that river, and found a pile of newly
gnawed sticks and twigs. The beaver works
with the cold-chisel, and a few clean strokes
suffice to level a four-inch bole. Across the
water on the far bank glimmered, with the
ghastly white of peeled dead timber, the
beaver-lodge—a mass of disheveled branches.
The inhabitants had dammed the stream lower
down and spread it into a nice little lake.
The question was would they come out for
their walk before it got too dark to see.
They came—blessings on their blunt muzzles,
they came—as shadows come, drifting down
the stream, stirring neither foot nor tail. There
were three of them. One went down to investigate the state of the dam ; the other two

began to look for supper. There is only one thing more startling than the noiselessness of a tiger in the jungle, and that is the noiselessness of a beaver in the water. The straining ear could catch no sound whatever till they began to eat the thick green river-scudge that they call beaver-grass. I, bowed among the logs, held my breath and stared with all my eyes. They were not ten yards from me, and they would have eaten their dinner in peace so long as I had kept absolutely still. They were dear and desirable beasts, and I was just preparing to creep a step nearer when that wicked old lady from Chicago clattered down the bank, an umbrella in her hand, shrieking : " Beavers, beavers ! Young man, whurr are those beavers ? Good Lord ! What was that now ? "

The solitary watcher might have heard a pistol shot ring through the air. I wish it had killed the old lady, but it was only the beaver giving warning of danger with the slap of his tail on the water. It was exactly like the " phink " of a pistol fired with damp powder. Then there were no more beavers—not a whisker-end. The lodge, however, was there, and a beast lower than any beaver began to throw stones at it because the old lady from Chicago said : " P'raps, if you rattle them up they'll come out. I do so want to see a beaver."

Yet it cheers me to think I have seen the beaver in his wilds. Never will I go to the

Zoo. That even, after supper—'twere flattery
to call it dinner—a Captain and a Subaltern
of the cavalry post appeared at the hotel.
These were the officers of whom the Mammoth Springs Captain had spoken. The
Lieutenant had read everything that he could
lay hands on about the Indian army, especially our cavalry arrangements, and was very
full of a scheme for raising the riding Red
Indians—it is not every noble savage that will
make a trooper—into frontier levies—a sort
of Khyber guard. "Only," as he said ruefully, "there is no frontier these days, and all
our Indian wars are nearly over. Those
beautiful beasts will die out, and nobody will
ever know what splendid cavalry they can
make."

The Captain told stories of Border warfare
—of ambush, firing on the rear-guard, heat
that split the skull better than any tomahawk,
cold that wrinkled the very liver, night-stampedes of baggage-mules, raiding of cattle,
and hopeless stern-chases into inhospitable
hills, when the cavalry knew that they were
not only being outpaced but outspied. Then
he spoke of one fair charge when a tribe gave
battle in the open and the troopers rode in
swordless, firing right and left with their revolvers and—it was excessively uncomfy for
that tribe. And I spoke of what men had
told me of huntings in Burma, of hill-climbing
in the Black Mountain affair, and so forth.

"Exactly!" said the Captain. "Nobody knows and nobody cares. What does it matter to the Down-Easter who Wrap-up-his-Tail was?"

"And what does the fat Briton know or care about Boh Hla-Oo?" said I. Then both together: "Depend upon it, my dear, Sir, the army in both Anglo-Saxon countries is a mischievously underestimated institution, and it's a pleasure to meet a man who," etc., etc. And we nodded triangularly in all good will, and swore eternal friendship. · The Lieutenant made a statement which rather amazed me. He said that, on account of the scarcity of business, many American officers were to be found getting practical instruction from little troubles among the South American Republics. When the need broke out they would return. "There is so little for us to do, and the Republic has a trick of making us hedge and ditch for our pay. A little road-making on service is not a bad thing, but continuous navvying is enough to knock the heart out of any army."

I agreed, and we sat up till two in the morning swapping the lies of East and West. As that glorious chief Man-afraid-of-Pink-Rats once said to the Agent on the Reservation: "'Melican officer good man. Heap good man. Drink me. Drink he. Drink me. Drink he. Drink *he*. Me blind. *Heap* good man!"

X.

"What man would read and read the selfsame faces
And like the marbles which the windmill grinds,
Rub smooth forever with the same smooth minds,
This year retracing last year's every year's dull
    traces,
Where there are woods and unmanstifled places?"
                                    —*Lowell.*

ONCE upon a time there was a carter who
brought his team and a friend into the Yellowstone Park without due thought.   Presently
they came upon a few of the natural beauties
of the place, and that carter turned his team
into his friend's team howling: "Get back o'
this, Jim.   All Hell's alight under our noses."
And they call the place Hell's Half-acre to
this day.   We, too, the old lady from Chicago,
her husband, Tom, and the good little mares
came to Hell's Half-acre, which is about sixty
acres, and when Tom said: "Would you like
to drive over it?" we said: "Certainly no,
and if you do, we shall report you to the
authorities."   There was a plain, blistered
and peeled and abominable, and it was given
over to the sportings and spoutings of devils
who threw mud and steam and dirt at each
other with whoops and halloos and bellowing
curses.   The place smelt of the refuse of the
Pit, and that odor mixed with the clean,

wholesome aroma of the pines in our nostrils
throughout the day.   Be it known that the
Park is laid out, like Ollendorf, in exercises
of progressive difficulty.   Hell's Half-acre
was a prelude to ten or twelve miles of geyser
formation.   We passed hot streams boiling in
the forest ; saw whiffs of steam beyond these,
and yet other whiffs breaking through the
misty green hills in the far distance ; we
trampled on sulphur, and sniffed things much
worse than any sulphur which is known to the
upper world ; and so came upon a parklike
place where Tom suggested we should get out
and play with the geysers.

Imagine mighty green fields splattered with
lime beds : all the flowers of the summer
growing up to the very edge of the lime.
That was the first glimpse of the geyser
basins.   The buggy had pulled up close to a
rough, broken, blistered cone of stuff between
ten and twenty feet high.   There was trouble
in that place—moaning, splashing, gurgling,
and the clank of machinery.   A spurt of boiling water jumped into the air and a wash
of water followed.   I removed swiftly.   The
old lady from Chicago shrieked.   "What a
wicked waste !" said her husband.   I think
they call it the Riverside Geyser.   Its spout
was torn and ragged like the mouth of a gun
when a shell has burst there.   It grumbled
madly for a moment or two and then was
still.   I crept over the steaming lime—it was

the burning marl on which Satan lay—and looked fearfully down its mouth. You should never look a gift geyser in the mouth. I beheld a horrible slippery slimy funnel with water rising and falling ten feet at a time. Then the water rose to lip level with a rush and an infernal bubbling troubled this Devil's Bethesda before the sullen heave of the crest of a wave lapped over the edge and made me run. Mark the nature of the human soul! I had begun with awe, not to say terror. I stepped back from the flanks of the Riverside Geyser saying: "Pooh! Is that all it can do?" Yet for aught I knew the whole thing might have blown up at a minute's notice; she, he, or it being an arrangement of uncertain temper.

We drifted on up that miraculous valley. On either side of us were hills from a thousand to fifteen feet high and wooded from heel to crest. As far as the eye could range forward were columns of steam in the air, misshapen lumps of lime, most like preadamite monsters, still pools of turquoise blue, stretches of blue cornflowers, a river that coiled on itself twenty times, boulders of strange colors, and ridges of glaring, staring white.

The old lady from Chicago poked with her parasol at the pools as though they had been alive. On one particularly innocent-looking little puddle she turned her back for a mo-

ment, and there rose behind her a twenty-
foot column of water and steam. Then she
shrieked and protested that " she never
thought it would ha' done it," and the old
man chewed his tobacco steadily, and
mourned for steam power wasted. I em-
braced the whitened stump of a middle-sized
pine that had grown all too close to a hot
pool's lip, and the whole thing turned over
under my hand as a tree would do in a nightmare. From right and left came the trum-
petings of elephants at play. I stepped into
a pool of old dried blood rimmed with the
nodding cornflowers; the blood changed to
ink even as I trod! and ink and blood were
washed away in a spurt of boiling sulphurous
water spat out from the lee of a bank of flowers. This sounds mad, doesn't it?

A moonfaced trooper of German extraction
—never was Park so carefully patrolled—
came up to inform us that as yet we had not
seen any of the real geysers, that they were
all a mile or so up the valley, tastefully scattered round the hotel in which we would rest
for the night. America is a free country, but
the citizens look down on the soldier. *I* had
to entertain that trooper. The old lady from
Chicago would have none of him; so we
loafed along together, now across half-rotten
pine logs sunk in swampy ground, anon over
the ringing geyser formation, then knee-deep
through long grass.

" And why did you 'list ? " said I.

The moonfaced one's face began to work.
I thought he would have a fit, but he told me
a story instead—such a nice tale of a naughty
little girl who wrote love letters to two men at
once. She was a simple village wife, but a
wicked " Family Novelette " countess couldn't
have accomplished her ends better. She
drove one man nearly wild with her pretty
little treachery ; and the other man abandoned
her and came West to forget. Moonface was
that man. We rounded a low spur of hill,
and came out upon a field of aching snowy
lime, rolled in sheets, twisted into knots, riven
with rents and diamonds and stars, stretching
for more than half a mile in every direction.
In this place of despair lay most of the big
geysers who know when there is trouble in
Krakatoa, who tell the pines when there is
a cyclone on the Atlantic seaboard, and who
—are exhibited to visitors under pretty and
fanciful names. The first mound that I encountered belonged to a goblin splashing in
his tub. I heard him kick, pull a shower-
bath on his shoulders, gasp, crack his joints,
and rub himself down with a towel ; then he
let the water out of the bath, as a thoughtful
man should, and it all sank down out of sight
till another goblin arrived. Yet they called
this place the Lioness and the Cubs. It lies
not very far from the Lion, which is a sullen,
roaring beast, and they say that when it is

very active the other geysers presently follow
suit. After the Krakatoa eruption all the
geysers went mad together, spouting, spurting,
and bellowing till men feared that they would
rip up the whole field. Mysterious sympa
thies exist among them, and when the Giant
ess speaks (of her more anon) they all hold
their peace.

I was watching a solitary spring, when, far
across the fields, stood up a plume of spun
glass, iridescent and superb, against the sky.
"That," said the trooper, "is Old Faithful.
He goes off every sixty-five minutes to the
minute, plays for five minutes, and sends up
a column of water a hundred and fifty feet
high. By the time you have looked at all the
other geysers he will be ready to play."

So we looked and we wondered at the Beehive, whose mouth is built up exactly like a hive;
at the Turban (which is not in the least like a
turban); and at many, many other geysers,
hot holes, and springs. Some of them
rumbled, some hissed, some went off spas-
modically, and others lay still in sheets of
sapphire and beryl.

Would you believe that even these terrible
creatures have to be guarded by the troopers
to prevent the irreverent American from chip-
ping the cones to pieces, or worse still, making the geysers sick? If you take of soft-
soap a small barrelful and drop it down a
geyser's mouth, that geyser will presently be

forced to lay all before you and for days afterwards will be of an irritated and inconsistent
stomach.   When they told me the tale I was
filled with sympathy.   Now I wish that I had
stolen soap and tried the experiment on some
lonely little beast of a geyser in the woods.
It sounds so probable—and so human.

Yet he would be a bold man who would administer emetics to the Giantess.   She is flat-
lipped, having no mouth, she looks like a
pool, fifty feet long and thirty wide, and there
is no ornamentation about her.   At irregular
intervals she speaks, and sends up a column
of water over two hundred feet high to begin
with ; then she is angry for a day and a half
—sometimes for two days.   Owing to her
peculiarity of going mad in the night not
many people have seen the Giantess at her
finest ; but the clamor of her unrest, men say,
shakes the wooden hotel, and echoes like
thunder among the hills.   When I saw her
trouble was brewing.   The pool bubbled seriously, and at five-minute intervals, sank a
foot or two, then rose, washed over the rim,
and huge steam bubbles broke on the top.
Just before an eruption the water entirely dis-
appears from view.   Whenever you see the
water die down in a geyser-mouth get away
as fast as you can.   I saw a tiny little geyser
suck in its breath in this way, and instinct
made me retire while it hooted after me.

Leaving the Giantess to swear, and spit,

and thresh about, we went over to Old Faithful, who by reason of his faithfulness has
benches close to him whence you may comfortably watch. At the appointed hour we
heard the water flying up and down the
mouth with the sob of waves in a cave.
Then came the preliminary gouts, then a roar
and a rush, and that glittering column of
diamonds rose, quivered, stood still for a
minute. Then it broke, and the rest was a
confused snarl of water not thirty feet high.
All the young ladies—not more than twenty
—in the tourist band remarked that it was
"elegant," and betook themselves to writing
their names in the bottoms of shallow pools.
Nature fixes the insult indelibly, and the
after-years will learn that " Hattie," " Sadie,"
" Mamie," " Sophie," and so forth, have taken
out their hairpins, and scrawled in the face
of Old Faithful.

The congregation returned to the hotel to
put down their impressions in diaries and
note-books which they wrote up ostentatiously
in the verandas. It was a sweltering hot
day, albeit we stood somewhat higher than
the summit of Jakko, and I left that raw pine-
creaking caravanserai for the cool shade of a
clump of pine between whose trunks glimmered
tents. A batch of troopers came down the
road, and flung themselves across country
into their rough lines. Verily the 'Melican
cavalry-man *can* ride, though he keeps his

11

accouterments pig, and his horse cow-
fashion.

I was free of that camp in five minutes—
free to play with the heavy lumpy carbines,
to have the saddles stripped, and punch the
horses knowingly in the ribs. One of the
men had been in the fight with "Wrap-up-his-
Tail" before alluded to, and he told me how
that great chief, his horse's tail tied up in red
calico, swaggered in front of the United
States cavalry, challenging all to single com-
bat. But he was slain, and a few of his tribe
with him. "There's no use in an Indian,
anyway," concluded my friend.

A couple of cowboys—real cowboys, not the
Buffalo Bill article—jingled through the camp
amid a shower of mild chaff. They were on
their way to Cook City, I fancy, and I know
that they never washed. But they were picturesque ruffians with long spurs, hooded stir-
rups, slouch hats, fur weather-cloths over their
knees, and pistol-butts easy to hand.

"The cowboy's goin' under before long,"
said my friend. "Soon as the country's
settled up he'll have to go. But he's mighty
useful now. What should we do without the
cowboy?"

"As how?" said I, and the camp laughed.

"He has the money. We have the know-
how. He comes in in winter to play poker at
the military posts. *We* play poker—a few.
When he's lost his money we make him drunk

and let him go. Sometimes we get the wrong man." And he told a tale of an innocent cowboy who turned up, cleaned out, at a post, and played poker for thirty-six hours. But it was the post that was cleaned out when that long-haired Caucasian Ah Sin removed himself, heavy with everybody's pay, and declining the proffered liquor. "Naow," said the historian, "I don't play with no cowboy unless he's a little bit drunk first."

Ere I departed I gathered from more than one man that significant fact that *up to one hundred yards* he felt absolutely secure behind his revolver.

"In England, I understand," quoth a limber youth from the South, "in England a man aren't allowed to play with no firearms. He's got to be taught all that when he enlists. I didn't want much teaching how to shoot straight 'fore I served Uncle Sam. And that's just where it is. But you was talking about your horseguards now?"

I explained briefly some peculiarities of equipment connected with our crackest crack cavalry. I grieve to say the camp roared.

"Take 'em over swampy ground. Let 'em run around a bit an' work the starch out of 'em, an' then, Almighty, if we wouldn't plug 'em at ease I'd eat their horses!"

"But suppose they engaged in the open?" said I.

"Engage the Hades. Not if there was a

tree-trunk within twenty miles they *couldn't* engage in the open!"

Gentlemen, the officers, have you ever seriously considered the existence on earth of a cavalry who by preference would fight in timber? The evident sincerity of the proposition made me think hard as I moved over to the hotel and joined a party exploration, which, diving into the woods, unearthed a pit pool of burningest water fringed with jet black sand—all the ground near by being pure white. But miracles pall when they arrive at the rate of twenty a day. A flaming dragon-fly flew over the pool, reeled and dropped on the water, dying without a quiver of his gorgeous wings, and the pool said nothing whatever, but sent its thin steam wreaths up to the burning sky. I prefer pools that talk.

There was a maiden—a very trim maiden—who had just stepped out of one of Mr. James's novels. She owned a delightful mother and an equally delightful father, a heavy-eyed, slow-voiced man of finance. The parents thought that their daughter wanted change. She lived in New Hampshire. Accordingly, she had dragged them up to Alaska, to the Yosemite Valley, and was now returning leisurely *via* the Yellowstone just in time for the tail-end of the summer season at Saratoga. We had met once or twice before in the Park, and I had been amazed and amused at her critical commendation of the wonders that she saw. From that very resolute little mouth I received a lecture on American literature, the nature and inwardness of Washington society, the precise value of Cable's works as compared with " Uncle Remus " Harris, and a few other things that had nothing whatever to do with geysers, but were altogether delightful. Now an English maiden who had stumbled on a dust-grimed, lime-washed, sun-peeled, collarless wanderer come from and going to goodness knows where, would, her mother inciting her and her father brandishing his umbrella, have regarded him as a dissolute adventurer. Not so those delightful people from New Hampshire. They were good enough to treat me—it sounds almost incredible—as a human being, possibly respectable, probably not in immediate need of financial assistance. Papa talked pleasantly and to the point. The little maiden strove valiantly with the accent of her birth and that of her reading, and mama smiled benignly in the background.

Balance this with a story of a young English idiot I met knocking about inside his high collars, attended by a valet. He condescended to tell me that " you can't be too careful who you talk to in these parts," and stalked on, fearing, I suppose, every minute for his social chastity. Now that man was a barbarian (I took occasion to tell him so), for he comported himself after the manner of the head-hunters of Assam, who are at perpetual feud one with another.

You will understand that these foolish tales are introduced in order to cover the fact that this pen cannot describe the glories of the Upper Geyser basin. The evening I spent under the lee of the Castle Geyser sitting on a log with some troopers and watching a baronial keep forty feet high spouting hot water. If the Castle went off first, they said the Giantess would be quiet, and *vice versa;* and then they told tales till the moon got up and a party of campers in the woods gave us all something to eat.

Next morning Tom drove us on, promising new wonders. He pulled up after a few miles at a clump of brushwood where an army was drowning. I could hear the sick gasps and thumps of the men going under, but when I broke through the brushwood the hosts had fled, and there were only pools of pink, black, and white lime, thick as turbid honey. They shot up a pat of mud every minute or two, choking in the effort. It was an uncanny sight. Do you wonder that in the old days the Indians were careful to avoid the Yellowstone? Geysers are permissible, but mud is terrifying. The old lady from Chicago took a piece of it, and in half an hour it dried into lime-dust and blew away between her fingers. All *maya,*—illusion,—you see! Then we clinked over sulphur in crystals; there was a

waterfall of boiling water; and a road across
a level park hotly contested by the beavers.
Every winter they build their dam and flood
the low-lying land; every summer that dam is
torn up by the Government, and for half a
mile you must plow axle-deep in water, the
willows brushing into the buggy, and little
waterways branching off right and left. The
road is the main stream—just like the Bolan
line in flood. If you turn up a byway, there
is no more of you, and the beavers work your
buggy into next year's dam.

Then came soft, turfy forest that deadened
the wheels, and two troopers—on detachment
duty—came noiselessly behind us. One was
the Wrap-up-his-Tail man, and we talked merrily while the half-broken horses bucked about
among the trees till we came to a mighty hill
all strewn with moss agates, and everybody
had to get out and pant in that thin air. But
how intoxicating it was! The old lady from
Chicago clucked like an emancipated hen as
she scuttled about the road cramming pieces
of rock into her reticule. She sent me fifty
yards down the hill to pick up a piece of broken bottle which she insisted was moss agate.
"I've some o' that at home an' they shine.
You go get it, young feller."

As we climbed the long path the road grew
viler and viler till it became without disguise
the bed of a torrent; and just when things
were at their rockiest we emerged into a little

sapphire lake—but never sapphire was so
blue—called Mary's lake; and that between
eight and nine thousand feet above the sea.
Then came grass downs, all on a vehement
slope, so that the buggy following the new-
made road ran on to the two off-wheels mostly, till we dipped head-first into a ford, climbed
up a cliff, raced along a down, dipped again
and pulled up disheveled at "Larry's" for
lunch and an hour's rest. Only "Larry"
could have managed that school-feast tent on
the lonely hillside. Need I say that he was
an Irishman? His supplies were at their
lowest ebb, but Larry enveloped us all in the
golden glamour of his speech ere we had de-
scended, and the tent with the rude trestle-table
became a palace, the rough fare, delicacies of
Delmonico, and we, the abashed recipients of
Larry's imperial bounty. It was only later
that I discovered I had paid eight shillings
for tinned beef, biscuits, and beer, but on the
other hand Larry had said: "Will I go out
an' kill a buffalo?" And I felt that for me
and for me alone would he have done it.
Everybody else felt that way. Good luck go
with Larry!

"An' now you'll all go an' wash your
pocket-handkerchiefs in that beautiful hot
spring round the corner," said he. "There's
soap an' a washboard ready, an' 'tis not every
day that ye can get hot water for nothing."
He waved us large-handedly to the open

downs while he put the tent to rights. There was no sense of fatigue on the body or distance in the air. Hill and dale rode on the eyeball. I could have clutched the far-off snowy peaks by putting out my hand. Never was such maddening air. Why we should have washed pocket-handkerchiefs Larry alone knows. It appeared to be a sort of religious rite. In a little valley overhung with gay painted rocks ran a stream of velvet brown and pink. It was hot—hotter than the hand could bear— and it colored the boulders in its course.

There was the maiden from New Hampshire, the old lady from Chicago, papa, mama, the woman who chewed gum, and all the rest of them, gravely bending over a washboard and soap. Mysterious virtues lay in that queer stream. It turned the linen white as driven snow in five minutes, and then we lay on the grass and laughed with sheer bliss of being alive. This have I known once in Japan, once on the banks of the Columbia, what time the salmon came in and " California " howled, and once again in the Yellowstone by the light of the eyes of the maiden from New Hampshire. Four little pools lay at my elbow: one was of black water (tepid), one clear water (cold), one clear water (hot), one red water (boiling); my newly washed handkerchief covered them all. We marveled as children marvel.

" This evening we shall do the grand cañon of the Yellowstone ? " said the maiden.

" Together ? " said I ; and she said yes.

The sun was sinking when we heard the roar of falling waters and came to a broad river along whose banks we ran. And then— oh, then ! I might at a pinch describe the infernal regions, but not the other place. Be it known to you that the Yellowstone River has occasion to run through a gorge about eight miles long. To get to the bottom of the gorge it makes two leaps, one of about one hundred and twenty and the other of three hundred feet. I investigated the upper or lesser fall, which is close to the hotel. Up to that time nothing particular happens to the Yellowstone, its banks being only rocky, rather steep, and plentifully adorned with pines. At the falls it comes round a corner, green, solid, ribbed with a little foam and not more than thirty yards wide. Then it goes over still green and rather more solid than before. After a minute or two you, sitting upon a rock directly above the drop, begin to understand that something has occurred ; that the river has jumped a huge distance between solid cliff walls—and what looks like the gentle froth of ripples lapping the sides of the gorge below is really the outcome of great waves. And the river yells aloud ; but the cliffs do not allow the yells to escape.

That inspection began with curiosity and finished in terror, for it seemed that the whole world was sliding in chrysolite from under my feet. I followed with the others round the corner to arrive at the brink of the cañon: we had to climb up a nearly perpendicular ascent to begin with, for the ground rises more than the river drops. Stately pine woods fringe either lip of the gorge, which is—the Gorge of the Yellowstone.

All I can say is that without warning or preparation I looked into a gulf seventeen hundred feet deep with eagles and fish-hawks circling far below. And the sides of that gulf were one wild welter of color—crimson, emerald, cobalt, ochre, amber, honey splashed with port-wine, snow-white, vermilion, lemon, and silver-gray, in wide washes. The sides did not fall sheer, but were graven by time and water and air into monstrous heads of kings, dead chiefs, men and women of the old time. So far below that no sound of its strife could reach us, the Yellowstone River ran—a finger-wide strip of jade-green. The sunlight took those wondrous walls and gave fresh hues to those that nature had already laid there. Once I saw the dawn break over a lake in Rajputana and the sun set over the Oodey Sagar amid a circle of Holman Hunt hills. This time I was watching both performances going on below me —upside down you understand—and the colors were real! The cañon was burning like Troy town; but it would burn forever, and, thank goodness, neither pen nor brush could ever portray its splendors adequately. The Acad-

emy would reject the picture for a chromolith-
ograph. The public would scoff at the letter-
press for *Daily Telegraphese.* " I will leave
this thing alone," said I ; " 'tis my peculiar
property. Nobody else shall share it with
me." Evening crept through the pines that
shadowed us, but the full glory of the day
flamed in that cañon as we went out very
cautiously to a jutting piece of rock—blood-
red or pink it was—that overhung the deepest
deeps of all. Now I know what it is to sit
enthroned amid the clouds of sunset. Gid-
diness took away all sensation of touch or form;
but the sense of blinding color remained.
When I reached the mainland again I had
sworn that I had been floating. The maid
from New Hamsphire said no word for a very
long time. She then quoted poetry, which
was perhaps the best thing she could have
done.

" And to think that this show-place has been
going on all these days an' none of we ever
saw it," said the old lady from Chicago, with
an acid glance at her husband.

" No, only the Injuns," said he, unmoved ;
and the maiden and I laughed long. Inspi-
ration is fleeting, beauty is vain, and the power
of the mind for wonder limited. Though the
shining hosts themselves had risen choiring
from the bottom cf the gorge they would not
have prevented her papa and one baser than
himself from rolling stones down those stupen-

dous rainbow-washed slides. Seventeen hundred feet of steepest pitch and rather more than seventeen hundred colors for log or boulder to whirl through ! So we heaved things and saw them gather way and bound from white rock to red or yellow, dragging behind them torrents of color, till the noise of their descent ceased and they bounded a hundred yards clear at the last into the Yellowstone.

"I've been down there," said Tom that evening. "It's easy to get down if you're careful—just sit and slide ; but getting up is worse. An' I found, down below there, two rocks just marked with a pictur of the cañon. I wouldn't sell those rocks not for fifteen dollars."

And papa and I crawled down to the Yellowstone—just above the first little fall—to wet a line for good luck. The round moon came up and turned the cliffs and pines into silver ; a two-pound trout came up also, and we slew him among the rocks, nearly tumbling into that wild river.

*   *   *   *   *

Then out and away to Livingstone once more. The maiden from New Hampshire disappeared ; papa and mama with her disappeared. Disappeared, too, the old lady from Chicago and all the rest, while I thought of all that I had *not* seen—the forest of petrified trees with amethyst crystals in their black

hearts ; the great Yellowstone Lake where
you catch your trout alive in one spring and
drop him into another to boil him ; and most
of all of that mysterious Hoodoo region where
all the devils not employed in the geysers live
and kill the wandering bear and elk, so that
the scared hunter finds in Death Gulch piked
carcasses of the dead whom no man has
smitten. Hoodoo-land with the overhead
noises, the bird and beast and devil rocks, the
mazes and the bottomless pits,—all these things
I missed. On the return road Yankee Jim
and Diana of the Crossways gave me kindly
greeting as the train paused an instant before
their door, and at Livingstone whom should I
see but Tom the driver ?

" I've done with the Yellowstone and decided
to clear out East somewheres," said he,
" Your talkin' about movin' round so gay an'
careless made me kinder restless ; I'm movin'
out."

Lord forgive us for our responsibility one to
another !

" And your partner ? " said I.

" Here's him," said Tom, introducing a
gawky youth with a bundle ; and I saw those
two young men turn their faces to the East.

XI.

" A fool also is full of words : a man cannot tell what
shall be ; and what shall be after him who can tell ? "

It has just occurred to me with great force
that delightful as these letters are to myself
their length and breadth and depth may be
just the least little bit in the world wearisome
to you over there. I will compress myself
rigorously, though I should very much like to
deliver a dissertation on the American Army
and the possibilities of its extension.

The American Army is a beautiful little
army. Some day, when all the Indians are
happily dead or drunk, it ought to make the
finest scientific and survey corps that the
world has ever seen. It does excellent work
now, but there is this defect in its nature ; it
is officered, as you know, from West Point, but
the mischief of it is that West Point seems to
be created for the purpose of spreading a
general knowledge of military matters among
the people. A boy goes up to that institution,
gets his pass, and returns to civil life, so they
tell me, with a dangerous knowledge that he is
a sucking Moltke, and may apply his learning
when occasion offers. Given trouble, that
man will be a nuisance, because he is a

hideously versatile American to begin with, as
cock-sure of himself as a man can be, and
with all the racial disregard for human life to
back him through his demi-semi-professional
generalship.

In a country where, as the records of the
daily papers show, men engaged in a conflict
with police or jails are all too ready to adopt
a military formation, and get heavily shot in a
sort of cheap, half-instructed warfare instead
of being decently scared by the appearance of
the military, this sort of arrangement does not
seem wise.

The bond between the States is of amazing
tenuity. So long as they do not absolutely
march into the District of Columbia, sit on
the Washington statues, and invent a flag
of their own, they can legislate, lynch, hunt
negroes through swamps, divorce, railroad,
and rampage as much as ever they choose.
They do not need knowledge of their own
military strength to back their genial lawlessness.

That Regular Army, which is a dear little
army, should be kept to itself, blooded on detachment duty, turned into the paths of
science, and now and again assembled at
feasts of Freemasons and so forth.

It's too tiny to be a political power. The
immortal wreck of the Grand Army of the
Republic is a political power of the largest
and most unblushing description.

It ought not to help to lay the foundations
of an amateur military power that is blind
and irresponsible. . . .

Be thankful that the balance of this lecture
is suppressed, and with it the account of a
" shiveree " which I attended in Livingstone
City: and the story of the editor and the sub-
editor (the latter was a pet cougar, or mountain lion, who used, they said, skilfully to
sub-edit disputants in the office) of the Livingstone daily paper.

Omitting a thousand matters of first im-
portance, let me pick up the thread of things
on a narrow-gauge line that took me down to
Salt Lake. The run between Delhi and
Ahmedabad on a May day would have been
bliss compared to this torture. There was
nothing but glare and desert and alkali dust.
There was no smoking-accommodation. I
sat in the lavatory with the conductor and a
prospector who told stories about Indian
atrocities in the voice of a dreaming child—
oath following oath as smoothly as clotted
cream laps the mouth of the jug. I don't
think he knew he was saying anything out of
the way, but nine or ten of those oaths were
new to me, and one even made the conductor
raise his eyebrows.

" And when a man's alone mostly, leadin' "
his horse across the hills, he gets to talk aloud
to himself as it was," said the weather-worn
retailer of tortures. A vision rose before me

12

of this man trampling the Bannack City trail under the stars—swearing, always swearing.

Bundles of rags that were pointed out as Red Indians, boarded the train from time to time. Their race privileges allow them free transit on the platforms of the cars. They mustn't come inside of course, and equally of course the train never thinks of pulling up for them. I saw a squaw take us flying and leave us in the same manner when we were spinning round a curve. Like the Punjabi, the Red Indian gets out by preference on the trackless plain and walks stolidly to the horizon. He never says where he is going. . . .

Salt Lake. I am concerned for the sake of Mr. Phil Robinson, his soul. You will remember that he wrote a book called *Saints and Sinners* in which he proved very prettily that the Mormon was almost altogether an estimable person. Ever since my arrival at Salt Lake I have been wondering what made him write that book. On mature reflection, and after a long walk round the city, I am inclined to think it was the sun, which is very powerful hereabouts.

By great good luck the evil-minded train already delayed twelve hours by a burnt bridge, brought me to the city on a Saturday by way of that valley which the Mormons aver their efforts had caused to blossom like the rose. Some hours previously I had entered a new world where, in conversation, every one was either a Mormon or a Gentile. It is not seemly for a free and independent citizen to dub himself a Gentile, but the Mayor of Ogden—which is the Gentile city of the valley—told me that there must be some distinction between the two flocks.

Long before the fruit orchards of Logan or the shining levels of the Salt Lake had been reached that Mayor—himself a Gentile, and one renowned for his dealings with the Mormons—told me that the great question of the existence of the power within the power was being gradually solved by the ballot and by education.

"We have," quoth he, "hills round and about here, stuffed full of silver and gold and lead, and all Hell atop of the Mormon church can't keep the Gentile from flocking in when that's the case. At Ogden, thirty miles from Salt Lake, this year the Gentile vote swamped the Mormon at the Municipal elections, and next year we trust that we shall be able to repeat our success in Salt Lake itself. In that city the Gentiles are only one-third of the total population, but the mass of 'em are grown men, capable of voting. Whereas the Mormons are cluttered up with children. I guess as soon as we have purely Gentile officers in the township, and the control of the policy of the city, the Mormons will have to back down considerable. They're bound to

go before long.   My own notion is that it's
the older men who keep alive the opposition
to the Gentile and all his works.   The younger
ones, spite of all the elders tell 'em, *will* mix
with the Gentile, and read Gentile books,
and you bet your sweet life there's a holy influence working toward conversion in the kiss
of an average Gentile—specially when the
girl knows that he won't think it necessary
for her salvation to load the house up with
other women-folk.   I guess the younger generation are giving sore trouble to the elders.
What's that you say about polygamy ?   It's a
penal offense now under a Bill passed not
long ago.   The Mormon has to elect one wife
and keep to her.   If he's caught visiting any
of the others—do you see that cool and restful brown stone building way over there
against the hillside ?   That's the penitentiary.
He is sent there to consider his sins, and he
pays a fine, too.   But most of the police in
Salt Lake are Mormons, and I don't suppose
they are too hard on their friends.   I presoom
there's a good deal of polygamy practised on
the sly.   But the chief trouble is to get the
Mormon to see that the Gentile isn't the
doubly-damned beast that the elders repre-
sent.   Only get the Gentiles well into the
State, and the whole concern is bound to go
to pieces in a very little time."

And the wish being father to the thought,
" Why, certainly," said I, and began to take

in the valley of Deseret, the home of the
latter-day saints, and the abode perhaps of as
much misery as has ever been compressed
into forty years.   The good folk at home will
not understand, but you will, what follows.
You know how in Bengal to this day the
child-wife is taught to curse her possible co-
wife, ere yet she has gone to her husband's
house ?   And the Bengali woman has been
accustomed to polygamy for a few hundred
years.   You know, too, the awful jealousy between mother wife and barren behind the
purdah—the jealousy that culminates sometimes in the poisoning of the well-beloved
son ?   Now and again, an Englishwoman
employs a high-caste Mussulman nurse, and
in the offices of that hire women are apt to
forget the differences of color, and to speak
unreservedly as twin daughters under Eve's
curse.   The nurse tells very strange and
awful things.   She has, and this the Mormons count a privilege, been born into polygamy ; but she loathes and detests it from
the bottom of her jealous soul.   And to the
lot of the Bengali co-wife—" the cursed of the
cursed—the daughter of the dunghill—the
scald-head and the barren-mute " (you know
the rest of that sweet commination-service)—
one creed, of all the White creeds to-day,
deliberately introduces the white woman taken
from centuries of training, which have taught
her that it is right to control the undivided

heart of one man. To quench her most natural rebellion, that amazing creed and fantastic jumble of Mahometanism, the Mosaic law, and imperfectly comprehended fragments of Freemasonry, calls to its aid all the powers of a hell conceived and elaborated by coarse-minded hedgers and ditchers. A sweet view, isn't it?

All the beauty of the valley could not make me forget it. But the valley is very fair. Bench after bench of land, flat as a table against the flanks of the ringing hills, marks where the Salt Lake rested for a while as it sunk from an inland sea to a lake fifty miles long and thirty broad. Before long the benches will be covered with houses. At present these are hidden among the green trees on the dead flat of the valley. You have read a hundred times how the streets of Salt Lake City are very broad, furnished with rows of shade trees and gutters of fresh water. This is true, but I struck the town in a season of great drouth—that same drouth which is playing havoc with the herds of Montana. The trees were limp, and the rills of sparkling water that one reads about were represented by dusty, paved courses. Main Street appears to be inhabited by the commercial Gentile, who has made of it a busy, bustling thoroughfare, and, in the eye of the sun, swigs the ungodly lager and smokes the improper cigar all day long. For which I like him. At the head of Main Street stand the lions of the place ; the Temple and the Tabernacle, the Tithing House, and the houses of Brigham Young, whose portrait is on sale in most of the booksellers' shops. Incidentally it may be mentioned that the late Amir of Utah does not unremotely resemble His Highness the Amir of Afghanistan, whom these fortunate eyes have seen. And I have no desire to fall into the hands of the Amir. The first thing to be seen was, of course, the outward exponent of a creed. Armed with a copy of the Book of Mormon, for better comprehension, I went to form rash opinions. Some day the Temple will be finished. It was begun only thirty years ago, and up to date rather more than three million dollars and a half have been expended in its granite bulk. The walls are ten feet thick ; the edifice itself is about a hundred feet high ; and its towers will be nearly two hundred. And that is all there is of it, unless you choose to inspect more closely ; always reading the Book of Mormon as you walk. Then the wondrous puerility, of what I suppose we must call the design, becomes apparent. These men, directly inspired from on High, heaped stone on stone and pillar on pillar, without achieving either dignity, relief, or interest. There is, over the main door, some pitiful scratching in stone representing the all-seeing eye, the Masonic grip, the sun, moon, and stars, and, perhaps, other skittles. The flatness and meanness of the thing almost makes you weep when you look at the magnificent granite in blocks strewn abroad, and think of the art that three million dollars might have called in to the aid of the church. It is as though a child had said : " Let us draw a great, big, fine house—finer than any house that ever was,"—and in that desire had laboriously smudged along with a ruler and pencil, piling meaningless straight lines on compass-drawn curves, with his tongue following every movement of the inept hand. Then sat I down on a wheelbarrow and read the Book of Mormon, and behold the spirit of the book was the spirit of the stone before me. The estimable Joseph and Hyrum Smith struggling to create a new Bible, when they knew nothing of the history of Old and New Testament, and the inspired architect muddling with his bricks—they were brothers. But the book was more interesting than the building. It is written, and all the world has read, how to Joseph Smith an angel came down from Heaven with a pair of celestial gig-lamps, whereby he was marvelously enabled to interpret certain plates of gold scribbled over with dots and scratches, and discovered by him in the ground. Which plates Joseph Smith did translate — only he spelt the mysterious characters " caractors "—and out of the dots and scratches produced a volume of six hundred closely printed pages, containing the books of Nephi, first and second, Jacob, Enos, Jarom, Omni, Mormon, Mosiah, the Record of Zeniff, the book of Alma Helaman, the third of Nephi, the book of Ether (the whole thing is a powerful anæsthetic, by the way), and the final book of Mononi. Three men, of whom one I believe is now living, bear solemn witness that the angel with the spectacles appeared unto them ; eight other men swear solemnly that they have seen the golden plates of.the revelation ; and upon this testimony the book of Mormon stands. The Mormon Bible begins at the days of Zedekiah, King of Judah, and ends in a wild and weltering quagmire of tribal fights, bits of revelation, and wholesale cribs from the Bible. Very sincerely did I sympathize with the inspired brothers as I waded through their joint production. As a humble fellow-worker in the field of fiction, I knew what it was to get good names for one's characters. But Joseph and Hyrum were harder bestead than ever I have been ; and bolder men to boot. They created Teancum and Coriantumy Pahoran, Kishkumen, and Gadianton, and other priceless names which the memory does not hold ; but of geography they wisely steered clear, and were astutely vague as to the locality of places, because you see they were by no means certain what lay in the next county to their own. They marched and countermarched bloodthirsty armies across their pages ; and added new and amazing chapters to the records of the New Testament, and reorganized the heavens and the earth as it is always lawful to do in print. But they could not achieve style, and it was foolish of them to let into their weird Mosaic pieces of the genuine Bible whenever the laboring pen dropped from its toilsome parody to a sentence or two of vile, bad English or downright " penny dreadfulism."   " And Moses said unto the people of Israel : ' Great Scott ! what air you doing ? ' " There is no sentence in the Book of Mormon word for word like the foregoing ; but the general tone is not widely different.

There are the makings of a very fine creed about Mormonism.   To begin with, the Church is rather more absolute than that of Rome.   Drop the polygamy plank in the platform, but on the other hand deal lightly with certain forms of excess.   Keep the quality of the recruits down to a low mental level and see that the best of the agricultural science available is in the hands of the Elders, and you have there a first-class engine for pioneer work.   The tawdry mysticism and the borrowings from Freemasonry serve the low-caste Swede and the Dane, the Welshman and the Cornish cottar, just as well as a highly organized Heaven.

I went about the streets and peeped into

people's front windows, and the decorations upon the tables were after the manner of the year 1850. Main Street was full of country folk from the outside come in to trade with the Zion Mercantile Co-operative Institute. The Church, I fancy, looks after the finances of this thing, and it consequently pays good dividends. The faces of the women were not lovely. Indeed, but for the certainty that ugly persons are just as irrational in the matter of undivided love as the beautiful, it seemed that polygamy was a blessed institution for the women, and that only the spiritual power could drive the hulking, board-faced men into it. The women wore hideous garments, and the men seemed to be tied up with string. They would market all that afternoon, and on Sunday go to the praying-place. I tried to talk to a few of them, but they spoke strange tongues and stared and behaved like cows. Yet one woman, and not an altogether ugly one, confided to me that she hated the idea of Salt Lake City being turned into a show-place for the amusement of the Gentile.

"If we 'ave our own institutions, that ain't no reason why people should come 'ere and stare at us, his it?"

The dropped "h" betrayed her.

"And when did you leave England?" I said.

"Summer of '84. I am from Dorset," she

said. " The Mormon agents was very good
to us, and we was very poor. Now we're
better off—my father an' mother an' me."

" Then you like the State ? "

She misunderstood at first. " Oh, I ain't
livin' in the state of polygamy. Not me yet.
I ain't married. I like where I am. I've got
things o' my own—and some land."

" But I suppose you will——"

" Not me. I ain't like them Swedes an'
Danes. I ain't got nothing to say for or
against polygamy. It's the Elders' business,
an' between you an' me I don't think it's
going on much longer. You'll 'ear them in
the 'ouse to-morrer talkin' as if it was
spreadin' all over America. The Swedes
they think it *his*. I know it hisn't."

" But you've got your land all right."

" Oh, yes, we've got our land an' we never
say aught against polygamy o' course—father
an' mother an' me."

It strikes me that there is a fraud somewhere. You've never heard of the rice-
Christians, have you ?

I should have liked to have spoken to the
maiden at length, but she dived into the Zion
Co-op. and a man captured me, saying that it
was my bounden duty to see the sights of Salt
Lake. These comprised the egg-shaped
Tabernacle, the Beehive, and town houses of
Brigham Young ; the same great ruffian's
tomb with assorted samples of his wives sleep-

ing round him (just as the eleven faithful ones sleep round the ashes of Runjit Singh outside Fort Lahore), and one or two other curiosities. But all these things have been described by abler pens than mine. The animal-houses where Brigham used to pack his wives are grubby villas; the Tabernacle is a shingled fraud, and the Tithing House where all the revenue returns seem to be made, much resembles a stable. The Mormons have a paper currency of their own—ecclesiastical bank-notes which are exchanged for local produce. But the little boys of the place prefer the bullion of the Gentiles. It is not pleasant to be taken round a township with your guide stopping before every third house to say: "That's where Elder so and so kept Amelia Bathershins, his fifth wife—no, his third. Amelia she was took on after Keziah, but Keziah was the Elder's pet, an' he didn't dare to let Amelia come across Keziah for fear of her spilin' Keziah's beauty." The Mussulmans are quite right. The minute that all the domestic details of polygamy are discussed in the mouths of the people, that institution is ready to fall. I shook off my guide when he had told me his very last doubtful tale, and went on alone. An ordered peace and a perfection of quiet luxury is the note of the city of Salt Lake. The houses stand in generous and well-groomed grass-plots, none very much worse or better than their neighbors.

Creepers grow over the house fronts, and
there is a very pleasant music of wind among
the trees in the vast empty streets bringing a
smell of hay and the flowers of summer.

On a tableland overlooking all the city
stands the United States garrison of infantry
and artillery. The State of Utah can do
nearly anything it pleases until that much-to-
be-desired hour when the Gentile vote shall
quietly swamp out Mormonism ; but the garrison is kept there in case of accidents. The
big, shark-mouthed, pig-eared, heavy-boned
farmers sometimes take to their creed with
wildest fanaticism, and in past years have
made life excessively unpleasant for the Gentile when he was few in the land. But to-
day, so far from killing openly or secretly, or
burning Gentile farms, it is all the Mormon
dares do to feebly try to boycott the inter-
loper. His journals preach defiance to the
United States Government, and in the Tabernacle of a Sunday the preachers follow suit.
When I went down there the place was full of
people who would have been much better for
a washing. A man rose up and told them
that they were the chosen of God, the elect of
Israel, that they were to obey their priest, and
that there was a good time coming. I fancy
that they had heard all this before so many
times it produced no impression whatever ;
even as the sublimest mysteries of another
Faith lost salt through constant iteration.

They breathed heavily through their noses and stared straight in front of them—impassive as flatfish.

And that evening I went up to the garrison post—one of the most coveted of all the army commands—and overlooked the City of the Saints as it lay in the circle of its forbidding hills. You can speculate a good deal about the mass of human misery, the loves frustrated, the gentle hearts broken, and the strong souls twisted from the law of life to a fiercer following of the law of death, that the hills have seen. How must it have been in the old days when the footsore emigrants broke through into the circle and knew that they were cut off from hope of return or sight of friends—were handed over to the power of the friends that called themselves priests of the Most High? " But for the grace of God there goes Richard Baxter," as the eminent divine once said. It seemed good that fate did not order me to be a brick in the up-building of the Mormon church, that has so aptly established herself by the borders of a lake bitter, salt, and hopeless.

XII.

"Much have I seen,
Cities and men."

LET there be no misunderstanding about the matter. I love this People, and if any contemptuous criticism has to be done, I will do it myself. My heart has gone out to them beyond all other peoples; and for the life of me I cannot tell why. They are bleeding-raw at the edges, almost more conceited than the English, vulgar with a massive vulgarity which is as though the Pyramids were coated with Christmas-cake sugar-works. Cocksure they are, lawless and as casual as they are cocksure; but I love them, and I realized it when I met an Englishman who laughed at them. He proved conclusively that they were all wrong, from their tariff to their go-as-you-please Civil Service, and beneath the consideration of a true Briton.

"I admit everything," said I. "Their Government's provisional; their law's the notion of the moment; their railways are made of hairpins and match-sticks, and most of their good luck lives in their woods and mines and rivers and not in their brains; but for all that, they be the biggest, finest, and best people on the surface of the globe!

Just you wait a hundred years and see how
they'll behave when they've had the screw put
on them and have forgotten a few of the
patriarchal teachings of the late Mister George
Washington. Wait till the Anglo-American-
German-Jew—the Man of the Future—is
properly equipped. He'll have just the least
little kink in his hair now and again; he'll
carry the English lungs above the Teuton feet
that can walk forever ; and he will wave long,
thin, bony Yankee hands with the big blue
veins on the wrist, from one end of the earth to
the other. He'll be the finest writer, poet, and
dramatist, 'specially dramatist, that the world
as it recollects itself has ever seen. By virtue
of his Jew blood—just a little, little drop—
he'll be a musician and a painter too. At
present there is too much balcony and too
little Romeo in the life-plays of his fellow-
citizens. Later on, when the proportion is
adjusted and he sees the possibilities of his
land, he will produce things that will make the
effete East stare. He will also be a complex
and highly composite administrator. There
is nothing known to man that he will not be,
and his country will sway the world with one
foot as a man tilts a seesaw plank ! "

" But this is worse than the Eagle at its
worst. Do you seriously believe all that ? "
said the Englishman.

" If I believe anything seriously, all this I
most firmly believe. You wait and see.

13

Sixty million people, chiefly of English instincts, who are trained from youth to believe
that nothing is impossible, don't slink through
the centuries like Russian peasantry. They
are bound to leave their mark somewhere, and
don't you forget it."

But isn't it sad to think that with all Eter-
nity behind and before us we cannot, even
though we would pay for it with sorrow, filch
from the Immensities one hundred poor years
of life, wherein to watch the two Great Experiments ? A hundred years hence India and
America will be worth observing. At present
the one is burned out and the other is only just
stoking up. When I left my opponent there
was much need for faith, because I fell into
the hands of a perfectly delightful man whom
I had met casually in the street, sitting in a
chair on the pavement, smoking a huge cigar.
He was a commercial traveler, and his beat
lay through Southern Mexico, and he told me
tales, of forgotten cities, stone gods up to their
sacred eyes in forest growth, Mexican priests,
rebellions, and dictatorships, that made my hair
curl. It was he who dragged me forth to
bathe in Salt Lake, which is some fifteen miles
away from the city, and reachable by many
trains which are but open tram-cars. The
track, like all American tracks, was terrifying
in its roughness ; and the end of the journey
disclosed the nakedness of the accommodation. There were piers and band houses and

refreshment stalls built over the solid gray levels of the lake, but they only accentuated the utter barrenness of the place. Americans don't mix with their scenery as yet.

And " Have faith," said the commercial traveler as he walked into water heavy as quicksilver. " Walk ! " I walked, and I walked till my legs flew up and I had to walk as one struggling with a high wind, but still I rode head and shoulders above the water. It was a horrible feeling, this inability to sink. Swimming was not much use. You couldn't get a grip of the water, so I e'en sat me down and drifted like a luxurious anemone among the hundreds that were bathing in that place. You could wallow for three-quarters of an hour in that warm, sticky brine and fear no evil consequences ; but when you came out you were coated with white salt from top to toe. And if you accidentally swallowed a mouthful of the water, you died. This is true, because I swallowed half a mouthful and was half-dead in consequence.

The commercial traveler on our return journey across the level flats that fringe the lake's edge bade me note some of the customs of his people. The great open railway car held about a hundred men and maidens, " coming up with a song from the sea." They sang and they shouted and they exchanged witticisms of the most poignant, and comported themselves like their brothers and sisters over the seas—the 'Arries and 'Arriets of the older world. And there sat behind me two modest maidens in white, alone and unattended. To these the privileged youth of the car—a youth of a marvelous range of voice—proffered undying affection. They laughed, but made no reply in words. The suit was renewed, and with extravagant imagery ; the nearest seats applauding. When we arrived at the city the maidens turned and went their way up a dark tree-shaded street, and the boys elsewhere. Whereat, recollecting what the London rough was like, I marveled that they did not pursue. " It's all right," said the commercial traveler. " If they had followed—well, I guess some one would ha' shot 'em." The very next day on those very peaceful cars returning from the Lake some one was shot—dead. He was what they call a " sport," which is American for a finished " leg," and he had an argument with a police officer, and the latter slew him. I saw his funeral go down the main street. There were nearly thirty carriages, filled with doubtful men, and women not in the least doubtful, and the local papers said that deceased had his merits, but it didn't much matter, because if the Sheriff hadn't dropped him he would assuredly have dropped the Sheriff. Somehow this jarred on my sensitive feelings, and I went away, though the commercial traveler would fain have entertained me

in his own house, he knowing not my name.
Twice through the long hot nights we talked,
tilting up our chairs on the sidewalk, of the
future of America.

You should hear the Saga of the States
reeled off by a young and enthusiastic citizen
who had just carved out for himself a home,
filled it with a pretty little wife, and is preparing to embark on commerce on his own
account. I was tempted to believe that pistol-
shots were regrettable accidents and lawlessness only the top scum on the great sea of
humanity. I am tempted to believe that still,
though baked and dusty Utah is very many
miles behind me.

Then chance threw me into the arms of
another and very different commercial traveler, as we pulled out of Utah on our way to
Omaha *via* the Rockies. He traveled in
biscuits, of which more anon, and Fate had
smitten him very heavily, having at one stroke
knocked all the beauty and joy out of his poor
life. So he journeyed with a case of samples
as one dazed, and his eyes took no pleasure
in anything that he saw. In his despair he
had withdrawn himself to his religion,—he
was a Baptist,—and spoke of its consolation
with the artless freedom that an American
generally exhibits when he is talking about his
most sacred private affairs. There was a
desert beyond Utah, hot and barren as Mian
Mir in May. The sun baked the car-roof, and

the dust caked the windows, and through the dust and the glare the man with the biscuits bore witness to his creed, which seems to include one of the greatest miracles in the world —the immediate unforeseen, self-conscious redemption of the soul by means very similar to those which turned Paul to the straight path.

" You must experi*ence* religion," he repeated, his mouth twitching and his eyes black-ringed with his recent loss. "You must experi*ence* religion. You can't tell when you're goin' to get, or haow; but it will come—it will come, Sir, like a lightning stroke, an' you will wrestle with yourself before you receive full conviction and assurance."

" How long does that take ? " I asked reverently.

" It may take hours. It may take days. I knew a man in San Jo who lay under conviction for a month an' the he ̄ot the sperrit— as you *must* git it."

" And then ? "

" And then you are saved. You feel that, an' you kin endure anything," he sighed. " Yes, anything. I don't care what it is, though I allow that some things are harder than others."

" Then you have to wait for the miracle to be worked by powers outside yourself. And if the miracle doesn't work ? "

" But it *must*. I tell you it must. It comes to all who profess with faith."

I learned a good deal about that creed as the train fled on ; and I wondered as I learned. It was a strange thing to watch that poor human soul, broken and bowed by its loss, nerving itself against each new pang of pain with the iterated assurance that it was safe against the pains of Hell.

The heat was stifling. We quitted the desert and launched into the rolling green plains of Colorado. Dozing uneasily with every removable rag removed, I was roused by a blast of intense cold and the drumming of a hundred drums. The train had stopped. Far as the eye could range the land was white under two feet of hail—each hailstone as big as the top of a sherry-glass. I saw a young colt by the side of the track standing with his poor little fluffy back to the pitiless pelting. He was pounded to death. An old horse met his doom on the run. He galloped wildly towards the train, but his hind legs dropped into a hole half water and half ice. He beat the ground with his fore-feet for a minute and then rolling over on his side submitted quietly to be killed.

When the storm ceased, we picked our way cautiously and crippledly over a track that might give way at any moment. The Western driver urges his train much as does the Subaltern the bounding pony, and 'twould seem with an equal sense of responsibility. If a foot does go wrong, why there you are, don't

you know, and if it is all right, why all right
it is, don't you know.   But I would sooner be
on the pony than the train.

This seems a good place wherein to preach
on American versatility. When Mr. Howells
writes a novel, when a reckless hero dams a
flood by heaving a dynamite-shattered mountain into it, or when a notoriety-hunting
preacher marries a couple in a balloon, you
shall hear the great American press rise on its
hind legs and walk round mouthing over the
versatility of the American citizen. And he
is versatile—horribly so. The unlimited exercise of the right of private judgment (which,
by the way, is a weapon not one man in ten is
competent to handle), his blatant cocksure-
ness, and the dry-air-bred restlessness that
makes him crawl all over the furniture when
he is talking to you, conspire to make him
versatile. But what he calls versatility the
impartial bystander of Anglo-Indian extraction
is apt to deem mere casualness, and dangerous
casualness at that. No man can grasp the
inwardness of an employ by the light of pure
reason—even though that reason be republican.
He must serve an apprenticeship to one craft
and learn that craft all the days of his life if
he wishes to excel therein. Otherwise he
merely "puts the thing through somehow;"
and occasionally he doesn't. But wherein lies
the beauty of this form of mental suppleness?
Old man California, whom I shall love and

respect always, told me one or two anecdotes
about American versatility and its consequences that came back to my mind with dire-
ful force as the train progressed. We didn't
upset, but I don't think that that was the
fault of the driver or the men who made the
track. Take up—you can easily find them—
the accounts of ten consecutive railway catas-
trophes—not little accidents, but first-class
fatalities, when the long cars turn over, take
fire, and roast the luckless occupants alive.
To seven out of the ten you shall find appended
the cheerful statement: "The accident is
supposed to have been due the rails spreading."
That means the metals were spiked down to
the ties with such versatility that the spikes or
the tracks drew under the constant vibration
of the traffic, and the metals opened out. No
one is hanged for these little affairs.

We began to climb hills, and then we
stopped—at night in darkness, while men
threw sand under the wheels and crowbarred
the track and then "guessed" that we might
proceed. Not being in the least anxious to
face my Maker half asleep and rubbing my
eyes, I went forward to a common car, and
was rewarded by two hours' conversation with
the stranded, broken-down, husband-aban-
doned actress of a fourth-rate, stranded,
broken-down, manager-bereft company. She
was muzzy with beer, reduced to her last
dollar, fearful that there would be no one to

meet her at Omaha, and wept at intervals because she had given the conductor a five-
dollar bill to change, and he hadn't come back.
He was an Irishman, so I knew he couldn't
steal, and I addressed myself to the task of
consolation. I was rewarded, after a decent
interval, by the history of a life so wild, so
mixed, so desperately improbable, and yet so
simply probable, and above all so quick—not
fast—in its kaleidoscopic changes that the
Pioneer would reject any summary of it. And
so you will never know how she, the beery
woman with the tangled blond hair, was once
a girl on a farm in far-off New Jersey.
How he, a traveling actor, had wooed and
won her,—"but Paw he was always set
against Alf,"—and how he and she embarked
all their little capital on the word of a faith-
less manager who disbanded his company a
hundred miles from nowhere, and how she
and Alf and a third person who had not
yet made any noise in the world, had to
walk the railway-track and beg from the farm-
houses; how that third person arrived and
went away again with a wail, and how Alf
took to the whisky and other things still more
calculated to make a wife unhappy; and how
after barn-stormings, insults, shooting-scrapes,
and pitiful collapses of poor companies she
had once won an encore. It was not a cheerful tale to listen to. There was a real actress in the Pullman,—such an one as travels

sumptuously with a maid and dressing-case,
—and my draggle-tail thought of appealing to
her for help, but broke down after several attempts to walk into the car jauntily as befitted
a sister in the profession. Then the conductor reappeared,—the five-dollar bill honestly changed,—and she wept by reason of
beer and gratitude together, and then fell
asleep waveringly, alone in the car, and became almost beautiful and quite kissable;
while the Man with the Sorrow stood at
the door between actress and actress and
preached grim sermons on the certain end of
each if they did not mend their ways and
find regeneration through the miracle of the
Baptist creed. Yes, we were a queer company going up to the Rockies together. I
was the luckiest, because when a breakdown
occurred, and we were delayed for twelve
hours, I ate all the Baptist's sample-biscuits.
They were various in composition, but nourishing. Always travel with a " drummer."

XIII.

AFTER much dallying and more climbing we came to a pass like all the Bolan Passes in the world, and the Black Cañon of the Gunnison called they it. We had been climbing for very many hours, and attained a modest elevation of some seven or eight thousand feet above the sea, when we entered a gorge, remote from the sun, where the rocks were two thousand feet sheer, and where a rock-splintered river roared and howled ten feet below a track which seemed to have been built on the simple principle of dropping miscellaneous dirt into the river and pinning a few rails a-top. There was a glory and a wonder and a mystery about that mad ride which I felt keenly (you will find it properly dressed up in the guide-books), until I had to offer prayers for the safety of the train. There was no hope of seeing the track two hundred yards ahead. We seemed to be running into the bowels of the earth at the invitation of an irresponsible stream. Then the solid rock would open and disclose a curve of awful twistfulness. Then the driver put on all steam, and we would go round that curve on one wheel chiefly, the Gunnison River gnashing its teeth below. The cars overhung the edge of the water, and if a single one of the rails had chosen to spread, nothing in the wide world could have saved us from drowning. I knew we should damage something in the end—the somber horrors of the gorge, the rush of the jade-green water below, and the cheerful tales told by the conductor made me certain of the catastrophe.

We had just cleared the Black Cañon and another gorge, and were sailing out into open country nine thousand feet above the level of the sea, when we came most suddenly round a corner upon a causeway across a waste water—half dam and half quarry-pool. The locomotive gave one wild "Hoo! Hoo! Hoo!" but it was too late. He was a beautiful bull, and goodness only knows why he had chosen the track for a constitutional with his wife. *She* was flung to the left, but the cow-catcher caught *him*, and turning him round, heaved him shoulder deep into the pool. The expression of blank, blind bewilderment on his bovine, jovine face was wonderful to behold. He was not angry. I don't think he was even scared, though he must have flown ten yards through the air. All he wanted to know was: "Will somebody have the goodness to tell a respectable old gentleman what in the world, or out of it, has occurred?" And five minutes later the stream that had been snapping at our heels in the gorges split itself into a dozen silver threads on a breezy

upland, and became an innocent trout beck,
and we halted at a half-dead city, the name of
which does not remain with me. It had
originally been built on the crest of a wave of
prosperity. Once ten thousand people had
walked its street ; but the boom had collapsed.
The great brick houses and the factories were
empty. The population lived in little timber
shanties on the fringes of the deserted town.
There were some railway workshops and
things, and the hotel (whose pavement formed
the platform of the railway) contained one
hundred and more rooms—empty. The
place, in its half-inhabitedness, was more
desolate than Amber or Chitor. But a man
said : " Trout—six pounds—two miles away,"
and the Sorrowful Man and myself went in
search of 'em. The town was ringed by a
circle of hills all alive with little thunder-
storms that broke across the soft green of the
plain in wisps and washes of smoke and
amber.

To our tiny party associated himself a
lawyer from Chicago. We foregathered on
the question of flies, but I didn't expect to
meet Elijah Pogram in the flesh. He delivered orations on the future of England and
America, and of the Great Federation that
the years will bring forth when America and
England will belt the globe with their linked
hands. According to the notions of the
British, he made an ass of himself, but for all

his high-falutin he talked sense. I might knock through England on a four months' tour and not find a man capable of putting into words the passionate patriotism that possessed the little Chicago lawyer. And he was a man with points, for he offered me three days' shooting in Illinois, if I would step out of my path a little. I might travel for ten years up and down England ere I found a man who would give a complete stranger so much as a sandwich, and for twenty ere I squeezed as much enthusiasm out of a Britisher. He and I talked politics and trout-flies all one sultry day as we wandered up and down the shallows of the stream aforesaid. Little fish are sweet. I spent two hours whipping a ripple for a fish that I knew was there, and in the pasture-scented dusk caught a three-pounder on a ragged old brown hackle and landed him after ten minutes' excited argument. He was a beauty. If ever any man works the Western trout-streams, he would do well to bring out with him the dingiest flies he possesses. The natives laugh at the tiny English hooks, but they hold, and duns and drabs and sober grays seem to tickle the æsthetic tastes of the trout. For salmon (but don't say that I told you) use the spoon—gold on one-side, silver on the other. It is as killing as is a similar article with fish of another calibre. The natives seem to use much too coarse tackle.

It was a search for a small boy who should
know the river that revealed to me a new
phase of life—slack, slovenly, and shiftless,
but very interesting.   There was a family in
a packing-case hut on the outskirts of the
town.   They had seen the city when it was on
the boom and made pretense of being the
metropolis of the Rockies; and when the
boom was over, they did not go.   She was
affable, but deeply coated with dirt; he was
grim and grimy, and the little children were
simply caked with filth of various descriptions.
But they lived in a certain sort of squalid
luxury, six or eight of them in two rooms;
and they enjoyed the local society.   It was
their eight-year-old son whom I tried to take
out with me, but he had been catching trout
all his life and "guessed he didn't feel like
coming," though I proffered him six shillings
for what ought to have been a day's pleasuring.
" I'll stay with Maw," he said, and from that
attitude I could not move him.   Maw didn't
attempt to argue with him.   " If he says he
won't come, he won't," she said, as though
he were one of the elemental forces of nature
instead of a spankable brat; and " Paw,"
lounging by the store, refused to interfere.
Maw told me that she had been a school-
teacher in her not-so-distant youth, but did
not tell me what I was dying to know—how
she arrived at this mucky tenement at the
back of beyond, and why.   Though preserv-

ing the prettiness of her New England speech, she had come to regard washing as a luxury. Paw chewed tobacco and spat from time to time. Yet, when he opened his mouth for other purposes, he spoke like a well-educated man. There was a story there, but I couldn't get at it.

Next day the Man with the Sorrow and myself and a few others began the real ascent of the Rockies ; up to that time our climbing didn't count. The train ran violently up a steep place and was taken to pieces. Five cars were hitched on to two locomotives, and two cars to one locomotive. This seemed to be a kind and thoughtful act, but I was idiot enough to go forward and watch the coupling-on of the two rear cars in which Cæsar and his fortunes were to travel. Some one had lost or eaten the regularly ordained coupling, and a man picked up from the tailboard of the engine a single iron link about as thick as a fetter-link watch-chain, and "guessed it would do." Get hauled up a Simla cliff by the hook of a lady's parasol if you wish to appreciate my sentiments when the cars moved uphill and the link drew tight. Miles away and two thousand feet above our heads rose the shoulder of a hill epauletted with the long line of a snow-tunnel. The first section of the cars crawled a quarter of a mile ahead of us, the track snaked and looped behind, and there was a black drop to the left. So we

14

went up and up and up till the thin air grew
thinner and the *chunk-chunk-chunk* of the
laboring locomotive was answered by the
oppressed beating of the exhausted heart.
Through the checked light and shade of the
snow tunnels (horrible caverns of rude tim-
bering) we ground our way, halting now and
again to allow a down-train to pass. One
monster of forty mineral cars slid past, scarce
held by four locomotives, their brakes screaming and chortling in chorus; and in the end,
after a glimpse at half America spread map-
wise leagues below us, we halted at the head
of the longest snow tunnel of all, on the crest
of the divide, between ten and eleven thousand feet above the level of the sea. The
locomotive wished to draw breath, and the
passengers to gather the flowers that nodded
impertinently through the chinks of the board-
ing. A lady passenger's nose began to bleed,
and other ladies threw themselves down on
the seats and gasped with the gasping train,
while a wind as keen as a knife-edge rioted
down the grimy tunnel.

Then, despatching a pilot-engine to clear
the way, we began the downward portion of
the journey with every available brake on,
and frequent shrieks, till after some hours we
reached the level plain, and later the city of
Denver, where the Man with the Sorrow went
his way and left me to journey on to Omaha
alone, after one hasty glance at Denver. The

pulse of that town was too like the rushing mighty wind in the Rocky Mountain tunnel. It made me tired because complete strangers desired me to do something to mines which were in mountains, and to purchase building blocks upon inaccessible cliffs ; and once, a woman urged that I should supply her with strong drinks. I had almost forgotten that such attacks were possible in any land, for the outward and visible signs of public morality in American towns are generally safe-guarded. For that I respect this people. Omaha, Nebraska, was but a halting-place on the road to Chicago, but it revealed to me horrors that I would not willingly have missed. The city to casual investigation seemed to be populated entirely by Germans, Poles, Slavs, Hungarians, Croats, Magyars, and all the scum of the Eastern European States, but it must have been laid out by Americans. No other people would cut the traffic of a main street with two streams of railway lines, each some eight or nine tracks wide, and cheer-fully drive tram-cars across the metals. Every now and again they have horrible railway crossing accidents at Omaha, but nobody seems to think of building an overhead-bridge. That would interfere with the vested interests of the undertakers.

Be blessed to hear some details of one of that class.

There was a shop the like of which I had

never seen before : its windows were filled
with dress-coats for men, and dresses for
women. But the studs of the shirts were
made of stamped cloth upon the shirt front,
and there were no trousers to those coats—
nothing but a sweep of cheap black cloth
falling like an abbé's frock. In the doorway
sat a young man reading Pollock's *Course of
Time*, and by that I knew that he was an
undertaker. His name was Gring, which is a
beautiful name, and I talked to him on the mysteries of his Craft. He was an enthusiast and
an artist. I told him how corpses were burnt
in India. Said he : " We're vastly superior.
We hold—that is to say, embalm—our dead.
So ! " Whereupon he produced the horrible
weapons of his trade, and most practically
showed me how you " held " a man back from
that corruption which is his birthright. " And
I wish I could live a few generations just to
see how my people keep. But I'm sure it's
all right. Nothing can touch 'em after *I*'ve
embalmed 'em." Then he displayed one of
those ghastly dress-suits, and when I laid a
shuddering hand upon it, behold it crumpled
to nothing, for the white linen was sewn on to
the black cloth and—there was no back to it !
That was the horror. The garment was a
shell. " We dress a man in that," said Gring,
laying it out tastily on the counter. " As you
see here, our caskets have a plate-glass window in front " (Oh me, but that window in

the coffin was fitted with plush like a brough-
am-window!), "and you don't see anything
below the level of the man's waistcoat. Consequently. . . ." He unrolled the terrible
cheap black cloth that falls down over the
stark feet, and I jumped back. "Of course
a man can be dressed in his own clothes if he
likes, but these are the regular things: and
for women look at this!" He took up the
body of a high-necked dinner-dress in sub-
dued lilac, slashed and puffed and bedeviled
with black, but, like the dress-suit, backless,
and below the waist turning to shroud.
"That's for an old maid. But for a young
girl we give white with imitation pearls round
the neck. That looks very pretty through
the window of the casket—you see there's a
cushion for the head—with flowers banked all
round." Can you imagine anything more
awful than to take your last rest as much of a
dead fraud as ever you were a living lie—to
go into the darkness one-half of you shaved,
trimmed and dressed for an evening party,
while the other half—the half that your friends
cannot see—is enwrapped in a flapping black
sheet?

I know a little about burial customs in
various places in the world, and I tried hard
to make Mr. Gring comprehend dimly the
awful heathendom that he was responsible for
—the grotesquerie—the giggling horror of it
all. But he couldn't see it. Even when he

showed me a little boy's last suit, he
couldn't see it. He said it was quite
right to embalm and trick out and hypo-
critically bedizen the poor innocent dead in
their superior cushioned and pillowed caskets
with the window in front.

Bury me cased in canvas like a fishing-rod,
in the deep sea ; burn me on a back-water of
the Hugli with damp wood and no oil ; pin
me under a Pullman car and let the lighted
stove do its worst; sizzle me with a fallen
electric wire or whelm me in the sludge of a
broken river dam ; but may I never go down
to the Pit grinning out of a plate-glass window, in a backless dress-coat, and the front
half of a black stuff dressing-gown ; not
though I were " held " against the ravage of
the grave for ever and ever.   Amen !

XIV.

" I know thy cunning and thy greed,
  Thy hard, high lust and wilful deed,
  And all thy glory loves to tell
  Of specious gifts material."

I HAVE struck a city,—a real city,—and they call it Chicago. The other places do not count. San Francisco was a pleasure-resort as well as a city, and Salt Lake was a phenomenon. This place is the first American city I have encountered. It holds rather more than a million people with bodies, and stands on the same sort of soil as Calcutta. Having seen it, I urgently desire never to see it again. It is inhabited by savages. Its water is the water of the Hugli, and its air is dirt. Also it says that it is the " boss " town of America.

I do not believe that it has anything to do with this country. They told me to go to the Palmer House, which is a gilded and mirrored rabbit-warren, and there I found a huge hall of tessellated marble, crammed with people talking about money and spitting about everywhere. Other barbarians charged in and out of this inferno with letters and telegrams in their hands, and yet others shouted at each other. A man who had drunk quite as much

as was good for him told me that this was
" the finest hotel in the finest city on God Almighty's earth." By the way, when an
American wishes to indicate the next county
or State he says, "God A'mighty's earth."
This prevents discussion and flatters his
vanity.

Then I went out into the streets, which are
long and flat and without end. And verily it
is not a good thing to live in the East for any
length of time. Your ideas grow to clash
with those held by every right-thinking white
man. I looked down interminable vistas
flanked with nine, ten, and fifteen storied
houses, and crowded with men and women,
and the show impressed me with a great horror. Except in London—and I have forgotten what London is like—I had never seen so
many white people together, and never such a
collection of miserables. There was no color
in the street and no beauty—only a maze of
wire-ropes overhead and dirty stone flagging
underfoot. A cab-driver volunteered to show
me the glory of the town for so much an hour,
and with him I wandered far. He conceived
that all this turmoil and squash was a thing to
be reverently admired ; that it was good to
huddle men together in fifteen layers, one
atop of the other, and to dig holes in the
ground for offices. He said that Chicago
was a live town, and that all the creatures
hurrying by me were engaged in business.

That is to say, they were trying to make
some money, that they might not die
through lack of food to put into their bel-
lies. He took me to canals, black as ink,
and filled with untold abominations, and bade
me watch the stream of traffic across the
bridges. He then took me into a saloon, and,
while I drank, made me note that the floor was
covered with coins sunk into cement. A
Hottentot would not have been guilty of this
sort of barbarism. The coins made an effect
pretty enough, but the man who put them
there had no thought to beauty, and therefore
he was a savage. Then my cab-driver showed
me business-blocks, gay with signs and studded
with fantastic and absurd advertisements of
goods, and looking down the long street so
adorned it was as though each vender stood
at his door howling : " For the sake of money,
employ or buy of *me* and me only ! " Have
you ever seen a crowd at our famine relief
distributions ? You know then how men leap
into the air, stretching out their arms above
the crowd in the hope of being seen ; while
the women dolorously slap the stomachs of
their children and whimper. I had sooner
watch famine-relief than the white man engaged in what he calls legitimate competition.
The one I understand. The other makes me
ill. And the cabman said that these things
were the proof of progress ; and by that I
knew he had been reading his newspaper,

as every intelligent American should. The
papers tell their readers in language fitted to
their comprehension that the snarling together
of telegraph wires, the heaving up of houses,
and the making of money is progress.

I spent ten hours in that huge wilderness,
wandering through scores of miles of these
terrible streets, and jostling some few hundred
thousand of these terrible people who talked
money through their noses. The cabman left
me : but after a while I picked up another man
who was full of figures, and into my ears he
poured them as occasion required or the big
blank factories suggested. Here they turned
out so many hundred thousand dollars' worth
of such and such an article ; there so many
million other things ; this house was worth so
many million dollars ; that one so many million more or less. It was like listening to a
child babbling of its hoard of shells. It was
like watching a fool playing with buttons. But
I was expected to do more than listen or
watch. He demanded that I should admire ;
and the utmost that I could say was : " Are
these things so ? Then I am very sorry for
you." That made him angry, and he said
that insular envy made me unresponsive. So
you see I could not make him understand.

About four and a half hours after Adam was
turned out of the garden of Eden he felt hungry, and so, bidding Eve take care that her
head was not broken by the descending fruit,

shinned up a cocoanut palm.   That hurt his
legs, cut his breast, and made him breathe
heavily, and Eve was tormented with fear lest
her lord should miss his footing and so bring
the tragedy of this world to an end ere the
curtain had fairly risen.   Had I met Adam
then, I should have been sorry for him.   To-
day I find eleven hundred thousand of his
sons just as far advanced as their father in the
art of getting food, and immeasurably inferior
to him in that they think that their palm-trees
lead straight to the skies.   Consequently I am
sorry in rather more than a million different
ways.   In our East bread comes naturally
even to the poorest by a little scratching or
the gift of a friend not quite so poor.   In less
favored countries one is apt to forget.   Then
I went to bed.   And that was on a Saturday
night.

Sunday brought me the queerest experience
of all—a revelation of barbarism complete.   I
found a place that was officially described as
a church.   It was a circus really, but that the
worshipers did not know.   There were flowers all about the building, which was fitted up
with plush and stained oak and much luxury,
including twisted brass candlesticks of severest
Gothic design.   To these things, and a congregation of savages, entered suddenly a
wonderful man completely in the confidence of
their God, whom he treated colloquially and
exploited very much as a newspaper reporter

would exploit a foreign potentate. But, un-
like the newspaper reporter, he never allowed
his listeners to forget that he and not He was
the center of attraction. With a voice of silver
and with imagery borrowed from the auction-
room, he built up for his hearers a heaven on
the lines of the Palmer House (but with all
the gilding real gold and all the plate-glass
diamond) and set in the center of it a loud-
voiced, argumentative, and very shrewd creation that he called God. One sentence at this
point caught my delighted ear. It was *apropos* of some question of the Judgment Day and
ran : " No ! I tell you God doesn't do business
that way." He was giving them a deity whom
they could comprehend, in a gold and jewel
heaven in which they could take a natural interest. He interlarded his performance with
the slang of the streets, the counter, and the
Exchange, and he said that religion ought to
enter into daily life. Consequently I presume
he introduced it *as* daily life—his own and the
life of his friends.

Then I escaped before the blessing, desiring
no benediction at such hands. But the persons who listened seemed to enjoy themselves,
and I understood that I had met with a popular preacher. Later on when I had perused
the sermons of a gentleman called Talmage
and some others, I perceived that I had been
listening to a very mild specimen. Yet that
man, with his brutal gold and silver idols, his

hands-in-pocket, cigar-in-mouth, and hat-on-the-back-of-the-head style of dealing with the sacred vessels would count himself spiritually quite competent to send a mission to convert the Indians. All that Sunday I listened to people who said that the mere fact of spiking down strips of iron to wood and getting a steam and iron thing to run along them was progress. That the telephone was progress, and the network of wires overhead was progress. They repeated their statements again and again. One of them took me to their city hall and board of trade works and pointed it out with pride. It was very ugly, but very big, and the streets in front of it were narrow and unclean. When I saw the faces of the men who did business in that building I felt that there had been a mistake in their billeting.

By the way, 'tis a consolation to feel that I am not writing to an English audience. Then should I have to fall into feigned ecstasies over the marvelous progress of Chicago since the days of the great fire, to allude casually to the raising of the entire city so many feet above the level of the lake which it faces, and generally to grovel before the golden calf. But you, who are desperately poor, and therefore by these standards of no account, know things, and will understand when I write that they have managed to get a million of men together on flat land, and that the bulk of these men appear to be lower than *mahajans* and not so companionable as a punjabi *jat* after harvest. But I don't think it was the blind hurry of the people, their argot, and their grand ignorance of things beyond their immediate interests that displeased me so much as a study of the daily papers of Chicago. Imprimis, there was some sort of dispute between New York and Chicago as to which town should give an exhibition of products to be hereafter holden, and through the medium of their more dignified journals the two cities were ya-hooing and hi-yi-ing at each other like opposition newsboys. They called it humor, but it sounded like something quite different. That was only the first trouble. The second lay in the tone of the productions. Leading articles which include gems such as : " Back of such and such a place," or " We noticed, Tuesday, such an event," or " don't " for " does not " are things to be accepted with thankfulness. All that made me want to cry was that, in these papers, were faithfully reproduced all the war-cries and " back-talk " of the Palmer House bar, the slang of the barbers' shops, the mental elevation and integrity of the Pullman-car porter, the dignity of the Dime Museum, and the accuracy of the excited fishwife. I am sternly forbidden to believe that the paper educates the public ?

Just when the sense of unreality and op-

pression were strongest upon me, and when I
most wanted help, a man sat at my side and
began to talk what he called politics. I had
chanced to pay about six shillings for a
traveling-cap worth eighteen pence, and he
made of the fact a text for a sermon. He said
that this was a rich country and that the people liked to pay two hundred per cent. on the
value of a thing. They could afford it. He
said that the Government imposed a protective
duty of from ten to seventy per cent. on foreign-
made articles, and that the American manufacturer consequently could sell his goods for
a healthy sum. Thus an imported hat would,
with duty, cost two guineas. The American
manufacturer would make a hat for seventeen
shillings and sell it for one pound fifteen. In
these things, he said, lay the greatness of
America and the effeteness of England.
Competition between factory and factory kept
the prices down to decent limits, but I was
never to forget that this people were a rich
people, not like the pauper Continentals, and
that they enjoyed paying duties. To my weak
intellect this seemed rather like juggling with
counters. Everything that I have yet purchased costs about twice as much as it would
in England, and when native-made is of inferior
quality. Moreover, since these lines were
first thought of I have visited a gentleman
who owned a factory which used to produce
things. He owned the factory still. Not a

man was in it, but he was drawing a handsome income from a syndicate of firms for keeping it closed in order that it might not produce things.   This man said that if protection were abandoned, a tide of pauper labor would flood the country, and as I looked at his factory I thought how entirely better it was to have no labor of any kind whatever, rather than face so horrible a future.   Meantime, do you remember that this peculiar country enjoys paying money for value not received.   I am an alien, and for the life of me cannot see why six shillings should be paid for eighteen-penny caps, or eight shillings for half-crown cigar-cases.   When the country fills up to a decently populated level a few million people who are not aliens will be smitten with the same sort of blindness.

But   my   friend's   assertion   somehow thoroughly suited the grotesque ferocity of Chicago.   See now and judge! In the village of Isser Jang on the road to Montgomery there be four *changar* women who winnow corn—some seventy bushels a year.   Beyond their hut lives Puran Dass, the money-lender, who on good security lends as much as five thousand rupees in a year. Jowala Singh, the *lohar*, mends the village plow—some thirty, broken at the share, in three hundred and sixty-five days; and Hukm Chund, who is letter-writer and head of the little club under the travelers' tree, generally keeps the village

posted in such gossip as the barber and the
midwife have not yet made public property.
Chicago husks and winnows her wheat by the
million bushels, a hundred banks lend hundreds of millions of dollars in the year, and
scores of factories turn out plow gear and
machinery by steam.   Scores of daily papers
do work which Hukm Chund and the barber
and the midwife perform, with due regard for
public opinion, in the village of Isser Jang.
So far as manufactures go, the difference between Chicago on the lake and Isser Jang on
the Montgomery road is one of degree only,
and not of kind.   As far as the understanding
of the uses of life goes Isser Jang, for all its
seasonal cholera, has the advantage over
Chicago.   Jowala Singh knows and takes care
to avoid the three or four ghoul-haunted fields
on the outskirts of the village ; but he is not
urged by millions of devils to run about all day
in the sun and swear that his plowshares
are the best in the Punjab ; nor does Puran
Dass fly forth in a cart more than once or
twice a year, and he knows, on a pinch, how
to use the railway and the telegraph as well as
any son of Israel in Chicago.   But this is
absurd.   The East is not the West, and these
men must continue to deal with the machinery
of life, and to call it progress.   Their very
preachers dare not rebuke them.   They gloss
over the hunting for money and the twice-
sharpened bitterness of Adam's curse by saying

that such things dower a man with a larger range of thoughts and higher aspirations. They do not say : " Free yourself from your own slavery," but rather, " If you can possibly manage it, do not set quite so much store on the things of this world." And they do not know what the things of this world are.

I went off to see cattle killed by way of clearing my head, which, as you will perceive, was getting muddled. They say every Englishman goes to the Chicago stock-yards. You shall find them about six miles from the city ; and once having seen them will never forget the sight. As far as the eye can reach stretches a township of cattle-pens, cunningly divided into blocks so that the animals of any pen can be speedily driven out close to an inclined timber path which leads to an elevated covered way straddling high above the pens. These viaducts are two-storied. On the upper story tramp the doomed cattle, stolidly for the most part. On the lower, with a scuffling of sharp hooves and multitudinous yells, run the pigs. The same end is appointed for each. Thus you will see the gangs of cattle waiting their turn—as they wait sometimes for days ; and they need not be distressed by the sight of their fellows running about in the fear of death. All they know is that a man on horse- back causes their next-door neighbors to move by means of a whip. Certain bars and

fences are unshipped, and, behold, that crowd
have gone up the mouth of a sloping tunnel
and return no more.   It is different with the
pigs.   They shriek back the news of the
exodus to their friends, and a hundred pens
skirl responsive.   It was to the pigs I first
addressed myself.   Selecting a viaduct which
was full of them, as I could hear though I
could not see, I marked a somber building
whereto it ran, and went there, not unalarmed
by stray cattle who had managed to escape
from their proper quarters.   A pleasant smell
of brine warned me of what was coming.   I
entered the factory and found it full of pork
in barrels, and on another story more pork
unbarreled, and in a huge room, the halves of
swine for whose use great lumps of ice
were being pitched in at the window.   That
room was the mortuary chamber where the
pigs lie for a little while in state ere they begin their progress through such passages as
kings may sometimes travel.   Turning a
corner and not noting an overhead arrangement of greased rail, wheel, and pulley, I ran
into the arms of four eviscerated carcasses, all
pure white and of a human aspect, being
pushed by a man clad in vehement red.
When I leaped aside, the floor was slippery
under me.   There was a flavor of farmyard in
my nostrils and the shouting of a multitude in
my ears.   But there was no joy in that shouting.   Twelve men stood in two lines—six

aside. Between them and overhead ran the
railway of death that had nearly shunted me
through the window. Each man carried a
knife, the sleeves of his shirt were cut off
at the elbows, and from bosom to heel he was
blood-red. The atmosphere was stifling as a
night in the Rains, by reason of the steam and
the crowd. I climbed to the beginning of
things and, perched upon a narrow beam,
overlooked very nearly all the pigs ever bred
in Wisconsin. They had just been shot out
of the mouth of the viaduct and huddled together in a large pen. Thence they were
flicked persuasively, a few at the time, into a
smaller chamber, and there a man fixed tackle
on their hinder legs so that they rose in the
air suspended from the railway of death. Oh!
it was then they shrieked and called on their
mothers and made promises of amendment,
till the tackle-man punted them in their backs,
and they slid head down into a brick-floored
passage, very like a big kitchen sink that was
blood-red. There awaited them a red man
with a knife which he passed jauntily through
their throats, and the full-voiced shriek became a sputter, and then a fall as of heavy
tropical rain. The red man who was backed
against the passage wall stood clear of the
wildly kicking hoofs and passed his hand over
his eyes, not from any feeling of compassion,
but because the spurted blood was in his eyes
and he had barely time to stick the next

arrival. Then that first stuck swine dropped, still kicking, into a great vat of boiling water, and spoke no more words, but wallowed in obedience to some unseen machinery, and presently came forth at the lower end of the vat and was heaved on the blades of a blunt paddle-wheel-thing which said, "Hough! Hough! Hough!" and skelped all the hair off him except what little a couple of men with knives could remove. Then he was again hitched by the heels to that said railway and passed down the line of the twelve men—each man with a knife—leaving with each man a certain amount of his individuality which was taken away in a wheelbarrow, and when he reached the last man he was very beautiful to behold, but immensely unstuffed and limp. Preponderance of individuality was ever a bar to foreign travel. That pig could have been in no case to visit you in India had he not parted with some of his most cherished notions.

The dissecting part impressed me not so mech as the slaying. They were so excessively alive, these pigs. And then they were so excessively dead, and the man in the dripping, clammy, hot passage did not seem to care, and ere the blood of such an one had ceased to foam on the floor, such another, and four friends with him, had shrieked and died. But a pig is only the Unclean animal—forbidden by the Prophet.

I was destined to make rather a queer dis-
covery when I went over to the cattle-
slaughter. All the buildings here were on a
much larger scale, and there was no sound of
trouble, but I could smell the salt reek of
blood before I set foot in the place. The
cattle did not come directly through the viaduct as the pigs had done. They debouched
into a yard by the hundred, and they were
big red brutes carrying much flesh. In the
center of that yard stood a red Texan steer
with a headstall on his wicked head. No
man controlled him. He was, so to speak,
picking his teeth and whistling in an open
byre of his own when the cattle arrived. As
soon as the first one had fearfully quitted the
viaduct, this red devil put his hands in his
pockets and slouched across the yard, no man
guiding him. Then he lowed something to
the effect that he was the regularly appointed
guide of the establishment and would show
them round. They were country folk, but
they knew how to behave ; and so followed
Judas some hundred strong, patiently, and
with a look of bland wonder in their faces. I
saw his broad back jogging in advance of
them, up a lime-washed incline where I was
forbidden to follow. Then a door shut, and
in a minute back came Judas with the air of
a virtuous plow-bullock and took up his
place in his byre. Somebody laughed across
the yard, but I heard no sound of cattle from

the big brick building into which the mob had disappeared. Only Judas chewed the cud with a malignant satisfaction, and so I knew there was trouble, and ran round to the front of the factory and so entered and stood aghast.

Who takes count of the prejudices which we absorb through the skin by way of our surroundings? It was not the spectacle that impressed me. The first thought that almost spoke itself aloud was: " They are killing kine; " and it was a shock. The pigs were nobody's concern, but cattle—the brothers of the Cow, the Sacred Cow—were quite otherwise. The next time an M. P. tells me that India either Sultanzies or Brahminizes a man, I shall believe about half what he says. It is unpleasant to watch the slaughter of cattle when one has laughed at the notion for a few years. I could not see actually what was done in the first instance, because the row of stalls in which they lay was separated from me by fifty impassable feet of butchers and slung carcasses. All I know is that men swung open the doors of a stall as occasion required, and there lay two steers already stunned, and breathing heavily. These two they pole-axed, and half raising them by tackle they cut their throats. Two men skinned each carcass, somebody cut off the head, and in half a minute more the overhead rail carried two sides of beef to their appointed place.

There was clamor enough in the operating room, but from the waiting cattle, invisible on the other side of the line of pens, never a sound. They went to their death, trusting Judas, without a word. They were slain at the rate of five a minute, and if the pig men were spattered with blood, the cow butchers were bathed in it. The blood ran in muttering gutters. There was no place for hand or foot that was not coated with thicknesses of dried blood, and the stench of it in the nostrils bred fear.

And then the same merciful Providence that has showered goods things on my path throughout sent me an embodiment of the city of Chicago, so that I might remember it forever. Women come sometimes to see the slaughter, as they would come to see the slaughter of men. And there entered that vermilion hall a young woman of large mold, with brilliantly scarlet lips, and heavy eyebrows, and dark hair that came in a " widow's peak " on the forehead. She was well and healthy and alive, and she was dressed in flaming red and black, and her feet (know you that the feet of American women are like unto the feet of fairies?) her feet, I say, were cased in red leather shoes. She stood in a patch of sunlight, the red blood under her shoes, the vivid carcasses tacked round her, a bullock bleeding its life away not six feet away from her, and the death factory roaring all round her. She looked curiously, with hard, bold eyes, and was not ashamed.

Then said I : " This is a special Sending. I have seen the City of Chicago." And I went away to get peace and rest.

XV.

IT is a mean thing and an unhandsome to "do" a continent in five-hundred-mile jumps. But after those swine and bullocks at Chicago I felt that complete change of air would be good. The United States at present hinge in or about Chicago, as a double-leaved screen hinges. To be sure, the tiny New England States call a trip to Pennsylvania "going west," but the larger-minded citizen seems to reckon his longitude from Chicago. Twenty years hence the center of population—that shaded square on the census map—will have shifted, men say, far west of Chicago. Twenty years later it will be on the Pacific slope. Twenty years after that America will begin to crowd up, and there will be some trouble. People will demand manufactured goods for their reduced-establishment households at the cheapest possible rates, and the cry that the land is rich enough to afford protection will cease with a great abruptness. At present it is the farmer who pays most dearly for the luxury of high prices. In the old days, when the land was fresh and there was plenty of it and it cropped like the garden of Eden, he did not mind paying. Now there is not so much free land, and the old acres are needing stimulants, which cost money, and the farmer, who pays for everything, is beginning to ask questions. Also the great American nation, which individually never shuts a door behind its noble self, very seldom attempts to put back anything that it has taken from Nature's shelves. It grabs all it can and moves on. But the moving-on is nearly finished and the grabbing must stop, and then the Federal Government will have to establish a Woods and Forests Department the like of which was never seen in the world before. And all the people who have been accustomed to hack, mangle, and burn timber as they please will object, with shots and protestations, to this infringement of their rights. The nigger will breed bounteously, and *he* will have to be reckoned with; and the manufacturer will have to be contented with smaller profits, and *he* will have to be reckoned with; and the railways will no longer rule the countries through which they run, and they will have to be reckoned with. And nobody will approve of it in the least.

Yes; it will be a spectacle for all the world to watch, this big, slashing colt of a nation, that has got off with a flying start on a freshly littered course, being pulled back to the ruck by that very mutton-fisted jockey Necessity. There will be excitement in America when a few score millions of " sovereigns " discover

that what they considered the outcome of
their own Government is but the rapidly di-
minishing bounty of Nature ; and that if they
want to get on comfortably they must tackle
every single problem from labor to finance
humbly, without gasconade, and afresh. But
at present they look "that all the to-morrows
shall be as to-day," and if you argue with
them they say that the Democratic Idea will
keep things going. They believe in that
Idea, and the less well-informed fortify themselves in their belief by curious assertions as
to the despotism that exists in England. This
is pure provincialism, of course; but it is
very funny to listen to, especially when you
compare the theory with the practise (pistol,
chiefly) as proven in the newspapers. I
have striven to find out where the central
authority of the land lies. It isn't at Washington, because the Federal Government can't
do anything to the States save run the mail
and collect a Federal tax or two. It isn't in
the States, because the townships can do as
they like; and it isn't in the townships, because these are bossed by alien voters or
rings of patriotic homebred citizens. And it
certainly is not in the citizens, because they
are governed and coerced by despotic power
of public opinion as represented by their
papers, preachers, or local society. I found
one man who told me that if anything went
wrong in this huge congress of kings,—if

there was a split or an upheaval or a smash,
—the people in detail would be subject to
the Idea of the sovereign people in mass.
This is a survival from the Civil War, when,
you remember, the people in a majority did
with guns and swords slay and wound the
people in detail. All the same, the notion
seems very much like the worship by the
savage of the unloaded rifle as it leans against
the wall.

But the men and women set Us an example
in patriotism. They believe in their land and
its future, and its honor, and its glory, and
they are not ashamed to say so. From the
largest to the least runs this same proud, passionate conviction to which I take off my hat
and for which I love them. An average English householder seems to regard his country
as an abstraction to supply him with police-
men and fire-brigades. The cockney cad
cannot understand what the word means.
The bloomin' toffs he knows, and the law,
and the soldiers that supply him with a spectacle in the Parks; but he would laugh in
your face at the notion of any duty being
owed by himself to his land. Pick an American of the second generation anywhere you
please—from the cab-rank, the porter's room,
or the plow-tail—'specially the plow-tail,—
and that man will make you understand in
five minutes that he understands what manner
of thing his Republic is. He might laugh at

a law that didn't suit his convenience, draw
your eye-teeth in a bargain, and applaud
'cuteness on the outer verge of swindling; but
you should hear him stand up and sing :—

> * My country 'tis of thee,
> Sweet land of liberty,
> Of thee I sing ! "

I have heard a few thousand of them engaged
in that employment.   I respect him.   There is
too much Romeo and too little balcony about
our National Anthem.   With the American
article it is all balcony.   There must be born
a poet who shall give the English *the* song of
their own, own country—which is to say, of
about half the world.   Remains then only to
compose the greatest song of all—The Saga
of the Anglo-Saxon all round the earth—a
pæan that shall combine the terrible slow
swing of the *Battle Hymn of the Republic*
(which, if you know not, get chanted to you)
with *Britannia needs no Bulwarks*, the skirl of
the *British Grenadiers* with that perfect quick-
step, *Marching through Georgia*, and at the
end the wail of the *Dead March*.   For We,
even We who share the earth between us as
no gods have ever shared it, we also are mortal in the matter of our single selves.   Will
any one take the contract ?

It was with these rambling notions that I
arrived at the infinite peace of the tiny township of Musquash on the Monongahela River.
The clang and tumult of Chicago belonged to

another world. Imagine a rolling, wooded, English landscape, under softest of blue skies, dotted at three-mile intervals with fat little, quiet little villages, or aggressive little manufacturing towns that the trees and the folds of the hills mercifully prevented from betraying their presence. The golden-rod blazed in the pastures against the green of the mulleins, and the cows picked their way home through the twisted paths between the blackberry bushes. All summer was on the orchards, and the apples—such apples as we dream of when we eat the woolly imitations of Kashmir —were ripe and toothsome. It was good to lie in a hammock with half-shut eyes, and, in the utter stillness, to hear the apples dropping from the trees, and the tinkle of the cowbells as the cows walked statelily down the main road of the village. Everybody in that restful place seemed to have just as much as he wanted; a house with all comfortable appliances, a big or little veranda wherein to spend the day, a neatly shaved garden with a wild wealth of flowers, some cows, and an orchard. Everybody knew everybody else intimately, and what they did not know, the local daily paper—a daily for a village of twelve hundred people !—supplied. There was a courthouse where justice was done, and a jail where some most enviable prisoners lived, and there were four or five churches of four or five denominations. Also it was impossible to buy openly any liquor in that little paradise. But—and this is a very serious *but* —you could by procuring a medical certificate get strong drinks from the chemist. That is the drawback of prohibition. It makes a man who wants a drink a shirker and a contriver, which things are not good for the soul of a man, and presently, 'specially if he be young, causes him to believe that he may just as well be hanged for a sheep as for a lamb; and the end of that young man is not pretty. Nothing except a rattling fall will persuade an average colt that a fence is not meant to be jumped over; whereas if he be turned out into the open he learns to carry himself with discretion. One heard a good deal of this same dread of drink in Musquash, and even the maidens seemed to know too much about its effects upon certain unregenerate youths, who, if they had been once made thoroughly, effectually, and persistently drunk—with a tepid brandy and soda thrust before their goose-fleshed noses on the terrible Next Morning—would perhaps have seen the futility of their ways. It was a sin by village canons to imbibe lager, though—*experto crede* —you can get dropsy on that stuff long before you can get drunk. "But what man knows his mind?" Besides, it was all their own affair.

The little community seemed to be as self-contained as an Indian village. Had the rest

of the land sunk under the sea, Musquash
would have gone on sending its sons to school
in order to make them "good citizens,"
which is the constant prayer of the true
American father, settling its own road-making,
local cesses, town-lot arbitrations, and internal
government by ballot and vote and due respect to the voices of the headmen (which is
the salvation of the ballot), until such time as
all should take their places in the cemetery
appointed for their faith. Here were Americans and no aliens—men ruling themselves
by themselves and for themselves and their
wives and their children—in peace, order,
and decency.

But what went straightest to this heart,
though they did not know it, was that they were
Methody folk for the most part—aye, Methody
as ever trod a Yorkshire Moor, or drove on a
Sunday to some chapel of the Faith in the
Dales. The old Methody talk was there, with
the discipline whereby the souls of the Just are,
sometimes to their intense vexation, made
perfect on this earth in order that they may
"take out their letters and live and die in
good standing." If you don't know the talk,
you won't know what that means. The discipline, or dis*cip*line, is no thing to be trifled
with, and its working among a congregation
depends entirely upon the tact, humanity, and
sympathy of the leader who works it. He,
knowing what youth's desires are, can turn

16

the soul in the direction of good, gently, instead of wrenching it savagely towards the
right path only to see it break away quivering
and scared. The arm of the Discipline is
long. A maiden told me, as a new and
strange fact and one that would interest a
foreigner, of a friend of hers who had once
been admonished by some elders somewhere
—not in Musquash—for the heinous crime of
dancing. She, the friend, did not in the least
like it. She would not. Can't you imagine
the delightful results of a formal wigging ad-
ministered by a youngish and austere elder
who was not accustomed to make allowances
for the natural dancing instincts of the young
of the human animal ? The hot irons that are
held forth to scare may also sear, as those
who have ever lain under an unfortunate ex-
position of the old Faith can attest.

But it was all immensely interesting—the
absolutely fresh, wholesome, sweet life that
paid due reverence to the things of the next
world, but took good care to get enough
tennis in the cool of the evening ; that concerned itself as honestly and thoroughly with
the daily round, the trivial task (and that same
task is anything but trivial when you are
" helped " by an American " help ") as with
the salvation of the soul. I had the honor of
meeting in the flesh, even as Miss Louisa
Alcott drew them, Meg and Joe and Beth and
Amy, whom you ought to know. There was

no affectation of concealment in their lives
who had nothing to conceal.   There were
many "little women" in that place, because,
even as is the case in England, the boys had
gone out to seek their fortunes.   Some were
working in the thundering, clanging cities,
others had removed in the infinite West,
and others had disappeared in the languid,
lazy South ; and the maidens waited their return, which is the custom of maidens all over
the world.   Then the boys would come back
in the soft sunlight, attired in careful raiment,
their tongues cleansed of evil words and dis-
courtesy.   They had just come to call—bless
their carefully groomed heads, so they had,—
and the maidens in white dresses glimmered
like ghosts on the stoop and received them
according to their merits.   Mama had nothing to do with this, nor papa either, for he
was down-town trying to drive reason into the
head of a land surveyor ; and all along the
shaded, lazy, intimate street you heard the
garden-gates click and clash, as the mood of
the man varied, and bursts of pleasant laughter where three or four—be sure the white
muslins were among them,—discussed a pic-
nic past or a buggy-drive to come.   Then the
couples went their ways and talked together
till the young men had to go at last on account of the trains, and all trooped joyously
down to the station and thought no harm of
it.   And, indeed, why should they?   From

her fifteenth year the American maiden moves among " the boys " as a sister among brothers. They are her servants to take her out riding,—which is driving,—to give her flowers and candy. The last two items are expensive, and this is good for the young man, as teaching him to value friendship that costs a little in cash and may necessitate economy on the cigar side. As to the maiden, she is taught to respect herself, that her fate is in her own hands, and that she is the more stringently bound by the very measure of the liberty so freely accorded to her. Wherefore, in her own language, " she has a lovely time " with about two or three hundred boys who have sisters of their own, and a very accurate perception that if they were unworthy of their trust a syndicate of other boys would probably pass them into a world where there is neither marrying nor giving in marriage. And so time goes till the maiden knows the other side of the house,—knows that a man is not a demi-god nor a mysteriously veiled monster, but an average, egotistical, vain, gluttonous, but on the whole, companionable sort of person, to be soothed, fed, and managed—knowledge that does not come to her sister in England till after a few years of matrimony. And then she makes her choice. The Golden Light touches eyes that are full of comprehension ; but the light is golden none the less, for she makes just the same sweet, irrational choices that an English girl does. With this advantage: she knows a little more, has experience in entertaining, insight into the businesses, employ, and hobbies of men, gathered from countless talks with the boys, and talks with the other girls who find time at those mysterious conclaves to discuss what Tom, Ted, Stuke, or Jack have been doing. Thus it happens that she is a companion, in the fullest sense of the word, of the man she weds, zealous for the interest of the firm, to be consulted in time of stress and to be called upon for help and sympathy in time of danger. Pleasant it is that one heart should beat for you; but it is better when the head above that heart has been thinking hard on your behalf, and when the lips, that are also very pleasant to kiss, give wise counsel.

When the American maiden—I speak now for the rank and file of that noble army—is once married, why, it is finished. She has had her lovely time. It may have been five, seven, or ten years according to circumstances. She abdicates promptly with startling speed, and her place knows her no more except as with her husband. The Queen is dead, or looking after the house. This same household work seems to be the thing that ages the American woman. She is infamously "helped" by the Irish trollop and the negress alike. It is not fair upon her, because she has to do three parts of the housework her-

self, and in dry, nerve-straining air the
" chores " are a burden.   Be thankful, oh my
people, for Mauz Baksh, Kadir Baksh, and
the *ayah* while they are with you.   They are
twice as handy as the unkempt slatterns of
the furnished apartments to which you will return, Commissioners though you be ; and five
times as clever as the Amelia Araminta Re-
bellia Secessia Jackson (colored) under whose
ineptitude and insolence the young American
housewife groans.   But all this is far enough
from peaceful, placid Musquash, and its
boundless cordiality, its simple, genuine hos-
pitality, and its—what's the French word that
just covers all?—*gra—gracieuseness*, isn't it ?
Oh, be good to an American wherever you
meet him.   Put him up for the club, and he
will hold you listening till three in the morning ; give him the best tent, and the gram-fed
mutton.   I have incurred a debt of salt that I
can never repay, but do you return it piece-
meal to any of that Nation, and the account
will be on my head till our paths in the world
cross again.   He drinks iced water just as we
do ; but he doesn't quite like our cigars.

And how shall I finish the tale ?   Would it
interest you to learn of the picnics in the hot,
still woods that overhang the Monongahela,
when those idiotic American buggies that
can't turn round got stuck among the brambles and all but capsized ; of boating in the
blazing sun on the river that but a little time

before had cast at the feet of the horrified
village the corpses of the Johnstown tragedy?
I saw one, only one, remnant of that terrible
wreck. He had been a minister. House,
church, congregation, wife, and children had
been swept away from him in one night of
terror. He had no employment; he could
have employed himself at nothing. But God
had been very good to him. He sat in the
sun and smiled a little weakly. It was in his
poor blurred mind that something had happened—he was not sure what it was, but un-
doubtedly something had occurred. One
could only pray that the light would never
return.

But there be many pictures on my mind.
Of a huge manufacturing city of three hundred
thousand souls lighted and warmed by natural
gas, so that the great valley full of flaming
furnaces sent up no smoke wreaths to the clear
sky. Of Musquash itself lighted by the same
mysterious agency, flares of gas eight feet long,
roaring day and night at the corners of the
grass-grown streets because it wasn't worth
while to turn them out ; of fleets of coal-flats
being hauled down the river on an interminable journey to St. Louis ; of factories nest-
ling in woods where all the ax-handles and
shovels in the world seemed to be manufactured daily ; and last, of that quaint forgotten
German community, the Brotherhood of Perpetual Separation who founded themselves

when the State was yet young and land cheap, and are now dying out because they will neither marry nor give in marriage and their recruits are very few. The advance in the value of land has almost smothered these poor old people in a golden affluence that they never desired. They live in a little village where the houses are built old Dutch fashion, with their front doors away from the road, and cobbled paths all about. The cloistered peace of Musquash is a metropolitan riot beside the hush of that village. And there is, too, a love-tale tucked away among the flowers. It has taken seventy years in the telling, for the brother and sister loved each other well, but they loved their duty to the brotherhood more. So they have lived and still do live, seeing each other daily, and separated for all time. Any trouble that might have been is altogether wiped out of their faces, which are as calm as those of very little children. To the uninitiated those constant ones resemble extremely old people in garments of absurd cut. But they love each other, and that seems to bring one back quite naturally to the girls and the boys in Musquash. The boys were nice boys—graduates of Yale of course ; you mustn't mention Harvard here—but none the less skilled in business, in stocks and shares, the boring for oil, and the sale of everything that can be sold by one sinner to another. Skilled, too, in baseball, big-shouldered, with straight eyes and

square chins—but not above occasional diver-
sion and mild orgies. They will make good
citizens and possess the earth, and eventually
wed one of the nice white muslin dresses.
There are worse things in this world than
being " one of the boys " in Musquash.

XVI.

You are a contemptible lot, over yonder. Some of you are Commissioners, and some Lieutenant-Governors, and some have the V. C., and a few are privileged to walk about the Mall arm in arm with the Viceroy; but *I* have seen Mark Twain this golden morning, have shaken his hand, and smoked a cigar—no, two cigars—with him, and talked with him for more than two hours! Understand clearly that I do not despise you; indeed, I don't. I am only very sorry for you, from the Viceroy downward. To soothe your envy and to prove that I still regard you as my equals, I will tell you all about it.

They said in Buffalo that he was in Hartford, Conn.; and again they said " perchance he is gone upon a journey to Portland; " and a big, fat drummer vowed that he knew the great man intimately, and that Mark was spending the summer in Europe—which information so upset me that I embarked upon the wrong train, and was incontinently turned out by the conductor three-quarters of a mile from the station, amid the wilderness of railway tracks. Have you ever, encumbered with great-coat and valise, tried to dodge diversely-minded locomotives when the sun was shining

in your eyes ? But I forgot that you have not
seen Mark Twain, you people of no account !

Saved from the jaws of the cowcatcher, me
wandering devious a stranger met.

" Elmira is the place. Elmira in the State
of New York—this State, not two hundred
miles away ; " and he added, perfectly un-
necessarily, " Slide, Kelley, slide."

I slid on the West Shore line, I slid till
midnight, and they dumped me down at the
door of a frowzy hotel in Elmira. Yes, they
knew all about " that man Clemens," but reckoned he was not in town ; had gone East
somewhere. I had better possess my soul in
patience till the morrow, and then dig up the
" man Clemens' " brother-in-law, who was interested in coal.

The idea of chasing half a dozen relatives
in addition to Mark Twain up and down a city
of thirty thousand inhabitants kept me awake.
Morning revealed Elmira, whose streets were
desolated by railway tracks, and whose suburbs
were given up to the manufacture of door-
sashes and window-frames. It was surrounded
by pleasant, fat, little hills, rimmed with timber and topped with cultivation. The Che-
mung River flowed generally up and down the
town, and had just finished flooding a few of
the main streets.

The hotel-man and the telephone man
assured me that the much-desired brother-in-
law was out of town, and no one seemed to

know where " the man Clemens " abode.
Later on I discovered that he had not sum-
mered in that place for more than nineteen
seasons, and so was comparatively a new arrival.

A friendly policeman volunteered the news
that he had seen Twain or " some one very
like him " driving a buggy the day before.
This gave me a delightful sense of nearness.
Fancy living in a town where you could see
the author of *Tom Sawyer*, or " some one very
like him," jolting over the pavements in a
buggy !

" He lives out yonder at East Hill," said
the policeman ; " three miles from here."

Then the chase began—in a hired hack, up
an awful hill, where sunflowers blossomed by
the roadside, and crops waved, and *Harper's
Magazine* cows stood in eligible and com-
manding attitudes knee-deep in clover, all
ready to be transferred to photogravure. The
great man must have been prosecuted by outsiders aforetime, and fled up the hill for
refuge.

Presently the driver stopped at a miserable,
little white wood shanty, and demanded
" Mister Clemens."

" I know he's a big-bug and all that," he
explained, " but you can never tell what sort
of notions those sort of men take into their
heads to live in, anyways."

There rose up a young lady who was sketching thistletops and golden rod, amid a plentiful supply of both, and set the pilgrims on the right path.

"It's a pretty Gothic house on the left-hand side a little way farther on."

"Gothic h——," said the driver. "Very few of the city hacks take this drive, specially if they know they are coming out here," and he glared at me savagely.

It was a very pretty house, anything but Gothic, clothed with ivy, standing in a very big compound, and fronted by a veranda full of chairs and hammocks. The roof of the veranda was a trellis-work of creepers, and the sun peeping through moved on the shining boards below.

Decidedly this remote place was an ideal one for work, if a man could work among these soft airs and the murmur of the long-eared crops.

Appeared suddenly a lady used to dealing with rampageous outsiders. "Mr. Clemens has just walked downtown. He is at his brother-in-law's house."

Then he was within shouting distance, after all, and the chase had not been in vain. With speed I fled, and the driver, skidding the wheel and swearing audibly, arrived at the bottom of that hill without accidents. It was in the pause that followed between ringing the brother-in-law's bell and getting an answer that it occurred to me for the first time

Mark Twain might possibly have other en-
gagements than the entertainment of escaped
lunatics from India, be they never so full of
admiration. And in another man's house—
anyhow, what had I come to do or say?
Suppose the drawing-room should be full of
people,—suppose a baby was sick, how was I
to explain that I only wanted to shake hands
with him?

Then things happened somewhat in this
order. A big, darkened drawing-room; a
huge chair; a man with eyes, a mane of grizzled hair, a brown mustache covering a mouth
as delicate as a woman's, a strong, square
hand shaking mine, and the slowest calmest,
levellest voice in all the world saying:—

"Well, you think you owe me something,
and you've come to tell me so. That's what
I call squaring a debt handsomely."

"Piff!" from a cob-pipe (I always said
that a Missouri meerschaum was the best smoking in the world), and, behold! Mark Twain
had curled himself up in the big armchair,
and I was smoking reverently, as befits one
in the presence of his superior.

The thing that struck me first was that he
was an elderly man; yet, after a minute's
thought, I perceived that it was otherwise,
and in five minutes, the eyes looking at me,
I saw that the gray hair was an accident of
the most trivial. He was quite young. I
was shaking his hand. I was smoking his

cigar, and I was hearing him talk—this man
I had learned to love and admire fourteen
thousand miles away.

Reading his books, I had striven to get an
idea of his personality, and all my precon-
ceived notions were wrong and beneath the
reality. Blessed is the man who finds no dis-
illusion when he is brought face to face with a
revered writer. That was a moment to be
remembered; the landing of a twelve-pound
salmon was nothing to it. I had hooked
Mark Twain, and he was treating me as
though under certain circumstances I might
be an equal.

About this time I became aware that he
was discussing the copyright question. Here,
so far as I remember, is what he said.
Attend to the words of the oracle through
this unworthy medium transmitted. You will
never be able to imagine the long, slow surge
of the drawl, and the deadly gravity of the
countenance, the quaint pucker of the body,
one foot thrown over the arm of the chair,
the yellow pipe clinched in one corner of the
mouth, and the right hand casually caressing
the square chin:—

"Copyright? Some men have morals, and
some men have—other things. I presume a
publisher is a man. He is not born. He is
created—by circumstances. Some publishers
have morals. Mine have. They pay me for
the English productions of my books. When

you hear men talking of Bret Harte's works
and other works and my books being pirated,
ask them to be sure of their facts. I think
they'll find the books are paid for. It was
ever thus.

" I remember an unprincipaled and formidable publisher. Perhaps he's dead now.
He used to take my short stories—I can't
call it steal or pirate them. It was beyond
these things altogether. He took my stories
one at a time and made a book of it. If I
wrote an essay on dentistry or theology or any
little thing of that kind—just an essay that
long (he indicated half an inch on his finger),
any sort of essay—that publisher would
amend and improve my essay.

" He would get another man to write some
more to it or cut it about exactly as his needs
required. Then he would publish a book
called *Dentistry by Mark Twain*, that little
essay and some other things not mine added.
Theology would make another book, and so on.
I do not consider that fair. It's an insult.
But he's dead now, I think. I didn't kill him.

" There is a great deal of nonsense talked
about international copyright. The proper
way to treat a copyright is to make it exactly
like real estate in every way.

" It will settle itself under these conditions. If Congress were to bring in a law
that a man's life was not to extend over a
hundred and sixty years, somebody would

laugh. That law wouldn't concern anybody.
The man would be out of the jurisdiction of
the court. A term of years in copyright
comes to exactly the same thing. No law
can make a book live or cause it to die before
the appointed time.

"Tottletown, Cal., was a new town, with a
population of three thousand—banks, fire-
brigade, brick buildings, and all the modern
improvements. It lived, it flourished, and it
disappeared. To-day no man can put his
foot on any remnant of Tottletown, Cal. It's
dead. London continues to exist. Bill Smith,
author of a book read for the next year or so
is real estate in Tottletown. William Shakespeare, whose works are extensively read, is
real estate in London. Let Bill Smith, equally
with Mr. Shakespeare now deceased, have as
complete a control over his copyright as he
would over his real estate. Let him gamble
it away, drink it away, or—give it to the
church. Let his heirs and assigns treat it in
the same manner.

"Every now and again I go up to Washington, sitting on a board to drive that sort of
view into Congress. Congress takes its ar-
guments against international copyright .de-
livered ready made, and—Congress isn't very
strong. I put the real-estate view of the case
before one of the Senators.

"He said : 'Suppose a man has written a
book that will live forever?'

17

" I said : ' Neither you nor I will ever live to see that man, but we'll assume it. What then ? '

" He said : ' I want to protect the world against that man's heirs and assigns, working under your theory.'

" I said : ' You think that all the world has no commercial sense. The book that will live forever can't be artificially kept up at inflated prices. There will always be very expensive editions of it and cheap ones issuing side by side.'

" Take the case of Sir Walter Scott's novels," Mark Twain continued, turning to me. " When the copyright notes protected them, I bought editions as expensive as I could afford, because I liked them. At the same time the same firm were selling editions that a cat might buy. They had their real estate, and not being fools, recognized that one portion of the plot could be worked as a gold mine, another as a vegetable garden, and another as a marble quarry. Do you see ? "

What I saw with the greatest clearness was Mark Twain being forced to fight for the simple proposition that a man has as much right to the work of his brains (think of the heresy of it !) as to the labor of his hands. When the old lion roars, the young whelps growl. I growled assentingly, and the talk ran on from books in general to his own in particular.

Growing bold, and feeling that I had a few

hundred thousand folk at my back, I demanded whether Tom Sawyer married Judge Thatcher's daughter and whether we were ever going to hear of Tom Sawyer as a man.

"I haven't decided," quoth Mark Twain, getting up, filling his pipe, and walking up and down the room in his slippers. "I have a notion of writing the sequel to *Tom Sawyer* in two ways. In one I would make him rise to great honor and go to Congress, and in the other I should hang him. Then the friends and enemies of the book could take their choice."

Here I lost my reverence completely, and protested against any theory of the sort, because to me at least, Tom Sawyer was real.

"Oh, he *is* real," said Mark Twain. "He's all the boy that I have known or recollect, but that would be a good way of ending the book"; then, turning round, "because, when you come to think of it, neither religion, training, nor education avails anything against the force of circumstances that drive a man. Suppose we took the next four and twenty years of Tom Sawyer's life, and gave a little joggle to the circumstances that controlled him. He would, logically and according to the joggle, turn out a rip or an angel."

"Do you believe that, then?"

"I think so. Isn't it what you call Kismet?"

"Yes; but don't give him two joggles and show the result, because he isn't your property any more. He belongs to us."

He laughed—a large, wholesome laugh—
and this began a dissertation on the rights of
a man to do what he liked with his own crea-
tions, which being a matter of purely profes-
sional interest, I will mercifully omit.

Returning to the big chair, he, speaking of
truth and the like in literature, said that an
autobiography was the one work in which a
man, against his own will and in spite of his
utmost striving to the contrary, revealed himself in his true light to the world.

" A good deal of your life on the Mississipi
is autobiographical, isn't it ? " I asked.

" As near as it can be—when a man is
writing to a book and about himself. But in
genuine autobiography, I believe it is impossible for a man to tell the truth about himself
or to avoid impressing the reader with the
truth about himself.

" I made an experiment once. I got a
friend of mine—a man painfully given to
speak the truth on all occasions—a man who
wouldn't dream of telling a lie—and I made
him write his autobiography for his own
amusement and mine. He did it. The manuscript would have made an octavo volume,
but—good, honest man that he was—in every
single detail of his life that I knew about he
turned out, on paper, a formidable liar. He
could not help himself.

" It is not in human nature to write the
truth about itself. None the less the reader

gets a general impression from an autobiography whether the man is a fraud or a good man. The reader can't give his reasons any more than a man can explain why a woman struck him as being lovely when he doesn't remember her hair, eyes, teeth, or figure. And the impression that the reader gets is a correct one."

"Do you ever intend to write an autobiography?"

"If I do, it will be as other men have done —with the most earnest desire to make myself out to be the better man in every little business that has been to my discredit; and I shall fail, like the others, to make my readers believe anything except the truth."

This naturally led to a discussion on conscience. Then said Mark Twain, and his words are mighty and to be remembered:—

"Your conscience is a nuisance. A conscience is like a child. If you pet it and play with it and let it have everything that it wants, it becomes spoiled and intrudes on all your amusements and most of your griefs. Treat your conscience as you would treat anything else. When it is rebellious, spank it—be severe with it, argue with it, prevent it from coming to play with you at all hours, and you will secure a good conscience; that is to say, a properly trained one. A spoiled one simply destroys all the pleasure in life. I think I have reduced mine to order. At least, I

haven't heard from it for some time. Perhaps I have killed it from over-severity. It's
wrong to kill a child, but, in spite of all I
have said, a conscience differs from a child
in many ways. Perhaps it's best when it's
dead."

Here he told me a little—such things as a
man may tell a stranger—of his early life and
upbringing, and in what manner he had been
influenced for good by the example of his
parents. He spoke always through his eyes,
a light under the heavy eyebrows; anon
crossing the room with a step as light as a
girl's, to show me some book or other; then
resuming his walk up and down the room,
puffing at the cob pipe. I would have given
much for nerve enough to demand the gift of
that pipe—value, five cents when new. I
understood why certain savage tribes ardently
desired the liver of brave men slain in com-
bat. That pipe would have given me, perhaps, a hint of his keen insight into the souls
of men. But he never laid it aside within
stealing reach.

Once, indeed, he put his hand on my shoulder. It was an investiture of the Star of
India, blue silk, trumpets, and diamond-stud-
ded jewel, all complete. If, hereafter, in the
changes and chances of this mortal life, I fall
to cureless ruin, I will tell the superintendent
of the workhouse that Mark Twain once put
his hand on my shoulder; and he shall give

me a room to myself and a double allowance
of paupers' tobacco.

" I never read novels myself," said he, " except when the popular persecution forces me
to—when people plague me to know what I
think of the last book that every one is reading."

" And how did the latest persecution affect
you ? "

" Robert ? " said he, interrogatively.

I nodded.

" I read it, of course, for the workmanship.
That made me think I had neglected novels
too long—that there might be a good many
books as graceful in style somewhere on the
shelves ; so I began a course of novel reading. I have dropped it now ; it did not
amuse me. But as regards Robert, the effect
on me was exactly as though a singer of
street ballads were to hear excellent music
from a church organ. I didn't stop to ask
whether the music was legitimate or necessary.
listened, and I liked what I heard. I am
peaking of the grace and beauty of the style."

" You see," he went on, " every man has
his private opinion about a book. But that is
my private opinion. If I had lived in the beginning of things I should have looked around
the township to see what popular opinion
thought of the murder of Abel before I openly
condemned Cain. I should have had my
private opinion, of course, but I shouldn't

have expressed it until I had felt the way.
You have my private opinion about that book.
I don't know what my public ones are ex-
actly. They won't upset the earth."

He recurled himself into the chair and
talked of other things.

" I spend nine months of the year at Hartford. I have long ago satisfied myself that
there is no hope of doing much work during
those nine months. People come in and call.
They call at all hours, about everything in the
world. One day I thought I would keep a
list of interruptions. It began this way :—

" A man came and would see no one but
Mr. Clemens. He was an agent for photogravure reproductions of Salon pictures. I
very seldom use Salon pictures in my books.

" After that man another man, who refused
to see any one but Mr. Clemens, came to
make me write to Washington about something. I saw him. I saw a third man, then a
fourth. By this time it was noon. I had grown
tired of keeping the list. I wished to rest.

" But the fifth man was the only one of the
crowd with a card of his own. He sent up
his card. 'Ben Koontz, Hannibal, Mo.' I
was raised in Hannibal. Ben was an old
schoolmate of mine. Consequently I threw
the house wide open and rushed with both
hands out at a big, fat, heavy man, who was
not the Ben I had ever known—nor anything
like him.

" ' But *is* it you, Ben ? ' I said. ' You've altered in the last thousand years.'

" The fat man said : ' Well, I'm not Koontz exactly, but I met him down in Missouri, and he told me to be sure and call on you, and he gave me his card, and '—here he acted the little scene for my benefit—' if you can wait a minute till I can get out the circulars—I'm not Koontz exactly, but I'm traveling with the fullest line of rods you ever saw.' "

" And what happened ? " I asked breathlessly.

" I shut the door. He was not Ben Koontz —exactly—not my old schoolfellow, but I had shaken him by both hands in love, and . . . I had been bearded by a lightning-rod man in my own house.

" As I was saying, I do very little work in Hartford. I come here for three months every year, and I work four or five hours a day in a study down the garden of that little house on the hill. Of course, I do not object to two or three interruptions. When a man is in the full swing of his work these little things do not affect him. Eight or ten or twenty interruptions retard composition."

I was burning to ask him all manner of impertinent questions, as to which of his works he himself preferred, and so forth ; but, standing in awe of his eyes, I dared not. He spoke on, and I listened, groveling.

It was a question of mental equipment that

was on the carpet, and I am still wondering whether he meant what he said.

" Personally, ˅ never care for fiction or story-books. What I like to read about are facts and statistics of any kind. If they are only facts about the raising of radishes, they interest me. Just now, for instance, before you came in "—he pointed to an encyclopædia on the shelves—" I was reading an article about ' Mathematics.' Perfectly pure mathematics.

" My own knowledge of mathematics stops at ' twelve times twelve,' but I enjoyed that article immensely. I didn't understand a word of it ; but facts, or what a man believes to be facts, are always delightful. That mathematical fellow believed in his facts. So do I. Get your facts first and "—the voice dies away to an almost inaudible drone—" then you can distort 'em as much as you please."

Bearing this precious advice in my bosom, I left ; the great man assuring me with gentle kindness that I had not interrupted him in the least. Once outside the door, I yearned to go back and ask some questions—it was easy enough to think of them now—but his time was his own, though his books belonged to me.

I should have ample time to look back to that meeting across the graves of the days. But it was sad to think of the things he had not spoken about.

In San Francisco the men of *The Call* told me many legends of Mark's apprenticeship in their paper five and twenty years ago; how he was a reporter delightfully incapable of reporting according to the needs of the day. He preferred, so they said, to coil himself into a heap and meditate until the last minute. Then he would produce copy bearing no sort of relationship to his legitimate work— copy that made the editor swear horribly, and the readers of *The Call* ask for more.

I should like to have heard Mark's version of that, with some stories of his joyous and variegated past. He has been journeyman printer (in those days he wandered from the banks of the Missouri even to Philadelphia), pilot cub and full-blown pilot, soldier of the South (that was for three weeks only), private secretary to a Lieutenant-Governor of Nevada (that displeased him), miner, editor, special correspondent in the Sandwich Islands, and the Lord only knows what else. If so experienced a man could by any means be made drunk, it would be a glorious thing to fill him up with composite liquors, and, in the language of his own country, "let him retrospect." But these eyes will never see that orgy fit for the gods!